MOMENTUM

MAXIMIZE CLARITY,
MANAGE DISTRACTIONS
& MINIMIZE RESISTANCE

How to Avoid Going in the Wrong Direction

MOMENTUM

SAM SILVERSTEIN

Published and distributed by
SOUND WISDOM
PO Box 310
Shippensburg, PA 17257-0310
717-530-2122

info@soundwisdom.com

www.soundwisdom.com

ISBN 13 TP: 978-1-64095-552-3

ISBN 13 eBook: 978-1-64095-553-0

For Worldwide Distribution, Printed in the USA

1 2 3 4 5 6 7 8 / 29 28 27 26 25

Acknowledgments

ALL SUCCESSFUL PROJECTS achieve their success through the unending efforts of a team. Momentum in the real world, as in this book, is no different.

I want to express my heartfelt thanks to my publisher, John Martin, and the entire team at Sound Wisdom. Your ongoing support and dedication have been instrumental in creating these beautiful books that get shared around the world.

I especially want to thank Arjun Rajan on my team for all the energy, care, and effort you put into this project.

And none of my books would be possible without my wife Renee's support and critical feedback.

Thank you!

Contents

1

UNDERSTANDING MOMENTUM

**Obstacles Are
Opportunities**

We Not Me

**The Science of
Momentum**

IT STARTED ON A MOUNTAINSIDE

I'M IN TRANSIT FROM GENEVA, Switzerland, back home to St. Louis, Missouri. For the past 11 days, I have traveled with my daughter, Allison. We toured castles, museums, and beautiful communities. We hiked for miles and miles each day. We sat and enjoyed the solitude of a moment on a bench in the shadow of the Matterhorn.

In Lugano, we ate the best pizza we had ever tasted. Throughout the trip, we shared several pots of fondue, each one better than the last.

But the most moving moment of the trip happened when we were driving down one of those crazy mountain switchback roads with hairpin turn after hairpin turn, where there were no guardrails and no margin for error.

We were driving down a mountainside when we came around a turn and encountered a motorcycle accident. There were two bikes crumpled on their sides and two men lying on the road. Gas was everywhere. As I slowed to a stop, I could see that one of the men was bleeding profusely. A woman was tending to this man, but it was obvious that he was in trouble. I rolled down the window and asked if they needed a doctor. Allison, by the way, is a board-certified pediatrician with a specialty in palliative care.

The woman said she was a doctor and that an ambulance and helicopter were on the way. Before I could finish the conversation, Allison shouted, "I have to go." And in that instant, Allison had her seatbelt off and was out the door. I drove about 100 yards down the road until I could find a spot to pull the car off the road and safely park.

It was a while before two emergency vehicles and the helicopter arrived. Up to that point, Allison and the other doctor had no real tools to work with, so they used items that the people in the cars around them had to slow the driver's bleeding.

Fifty-seven minutes later, Allison was helping place the two men on the helicopter. In that 57-minute period, Allison and the other doctor worked together feverishly to stabilize the seriously injured driver so he could be flown to the hospital. Allison could not speak the language nor understand the injured man or the others on the scene. The two doctors never even had time to exchange names. They just worked together to save this man's life.

Those words, "I have to go," continue to ring in my ears. Allison is a trained doctor. And even though she is not a trauma doctor, she knew what she *had* to do, and she did it. She had to do everything in her power to make a difference and help save that man's life. As a father, I was so incredibly proud and moved in that moment.

We all have things in our life that we simply *have* to do. We are meant to do them. We must do them. They are literally in our destiny. Momentum is what positions and enables us to do them.

Momentum is the continuous pursuit of what we have to do in service to others. This is part of living an accountable life.

Momentum is never just about us, our personal gain, or our success. Momentum is always about moving forward in our pursuits so that we are positioned to make the lives of the people around us better as we continue to grow through those gifts we share. When we move forward in service to others, somehow, we move forward in our goals, purpose, and mission. In doing so, we create incredible impact and influence.

Momentum is the continuous pursuit of what we have to do in service to others.

This book is about us, you and me, discovering how to always move forward in our pursuits. Sometimes, moving forward means making decisions and executing. Sometimes, moving forward means sitting on a bench, looking at the Matterhorn, and just breathing.

I want you to master the mindset and skill of Momentum. This is my gift to you.

OUR REALITY

At some point, most of us, including myself, are confused about whether we are going down the right path in life. Have I picked the right major? Am I in the right career? Should I keep doing what I am doing? Should I try something new? Is it too late for me to change my course?

These thoughts pop into our heads and lead us to second-guess everything that we have been doing. They slowly erode our confidence and mental peace, forcing us to constantly wonder if we are pursuing the wrong goals. But where do these ideas come from? What are their root causes?

Sometimes, they arise as a result of comparison. Comparison with colleagues, social media comparisons, and TV shows. Many times in life, we will come across certain people who look like they can accomplish anything. These people look like overnight successes—it seems like they started yesterday, and they are already so good at what they do. It looks natural and easy for them, while we personally struggle to do the same. We feel like it comes naturally to them, but it does not for us. However, we will soon realize that in these situations, we often look at where they are right now and neglect all the activities they must have done to get there.

All these sources of comparison can lead to us painting ourselves in a bad light and becoming confused and frustrated with where we are right now. And in times like these, we truly feel lost. We feel behind. Seeing people who started where we started yet are far ahead of where we are now, makes it seem as if we will never catch up. We picture ourselves in a race, and everyone else is already two laps ahead.

At this point, we may have voices in our heads saying, "I might as well stop running, for no matter how hard I try or how fast I run, I will never be able to reach those ahead of me." This type of mindset leads us to being frozen and stuck where we are. We become incapable of action because we start to internalize the belief that action is meaningless.

Sometimes, it is just fear—fear that we are not good enough, fear that we do not actually belong where we are currently. Impostor syndrome might keep us from ever taking the steps to do the things we want to do, talk to the people we want to talk to, or ask the questions we want to ask. Fear holds us in place and stops us from growing out of our shells. It might prevent us from daring even to peek out.

Fear holds us in place and stops us from growing.

Most importantly, the feeling that is consistent across everything that might hold us in place and root us in confusion is the feeling of being alone. The feeling that you are the only one who feels like this. That you are the only one who is so behind. The only one who does not understand. The only one who is scared, out of place, and lost. The only one who does not know what to do next. This feeling of being alone in your confusion and fear is what truly cements us in inaction and stops us from moving forward.

How do we get unstuck?

The first step is to realize that we are not the only ones; everyone around us has also gone through that phase. Even the people who look like they are naturally excellent at everything they do. Even the ones who seemingly achieved instant success. Even the people whom we look up to with so much admiration and who we think of as role models have had times in life when they have felt lost, confused, and scared. They may still feel like they are struggling, but we do not know or see it.

Realizing that we are not alone allows us to begin accepting ourselves for who we are. We might not be entirely happy with where we are right now, which is not bad. If you are always content with where you are, you will never seek change or growth to reach a better, higher place. However, this growth must come from a desire to achieve greater heights rather than a disdain for your current position in life, for good things stem from good emotions.

When we begin to realize that our current confusion is universal, it is time to think about what we really want. What do you want to achieve that you are unhappy you have not done yet? You might want to grow your business to the next level, get that job promotion you have been eyeing, get a 4.0 GPA, or maybe even just go out more to improve your social life. Maybe you simply want a better, more meaningful relationship with a spouse or partner. No matter how big or how small our goals may be, no matter how diverse they might seem, at the core of almost everything a person wants to achieve in this manner can often be boiled down to a simple yet powerful core idea: "I want to be better."

Realizing that we are not alone allows us to begin accepting ourselves for who we are.

The question then becomes, if we all want to be better, what is stopping us from actually doing it? What prevents us from doing what we want to do? Well, the obvious answer is that there are challenges. Some of the challenges are present even when deciding to do something! What we discussed earlier about realizing that we are not alone is a challenge in itself.

Perhaps the greatest challenge, and the hardest thing we can ever do, is simply to start. Start working on the goals and projects we want to work on. Start doing the activities and building the habits we know will improve our lives. Starting is the hardest challenge, which stops most of us in our tracks before the journey toward becoming who we want to be even starts.

The hardest thing to do is to start.

In addition, **the easiest thing for us to do in life is to do nothing**, to continue doing what we are used to, and to stay where we are. This happens to all of us multiple times every day—when we choose to hit snooze on our alarms rather than wake up for the morning jog, when we continue watching YouTube videos rather than reading that book, or even when we try to be productive by planning out the rest of the week rather than completing the report that we need to get done by tonight.

Inaction is the easiest thing to do, for you just let yourself slide down the current path you are on. To get onto the better path, you must lift yourself up and move, which requires effort, concentration, and dedication. This easiness of not doing anything is another challenge in itself.

The easiest thing for us to do in life is to do nothing.

On the other hand, we sometimes manage to somehow get started but often struggle to keep going forward to reach our goals. We might go to the gym for a week before we slack off and avoid it for a month. We might make our bed after waking up for a few days, but on that one day when we are in a rush, we do not. And since we did not make the bed today, we might also feel more inclined not to do it tomorrow. And soon, the habit of making your bed in the morning stops. This is because of two things that work against our progress and growth: *the second **hardest** thing to do is to keep going, and the second **easiest** thing to do is to stop.*

Well then, what do we even do? If we are surrounded by challenges in every direction, when starting itself is the biggest challenge, how do we ever get out of where we are right now? How do we get to where we want to be and truly grow as a person? Even though the question seems impossible, the answer is surprisingly simple. We just need to slightly shift our mindset.

What if our challenges are not really obstacles to our journey? What if we see them as something more powerful, something more empowering? Seeing our challenges for what they really are, opportunities, changes how our world works.

Our setbacks do not have to be walls that we let stop us on our way but rather steps that we need to learn to climb to grow higher. We freeze if we see something as an obstacle, a wall. We perceive it as so tall that we do not even go closer to examine it. Instead, we think, *There is a wall in my way, and my way forward is blocked.* We give up. We do not stop and think, *What if I have the skills to scale this wall? Should I go closer to see if there is maybe a way around it? What if there is a ladder lying around somewhere? Can I go under the wall to get past it?*

Seeing our challenges for what they really are, opportunities, changes the way our world works.

We do not consider these possibilities; for the moment we perceive it as this great wall stopping us from going forward, we give up. This can occur for many reasons. As discussed earlier, we might be scared of even checking out the wall because we are afraid that we are not good enough to climb it. Or maybe we have never seen this type of wall before, which prevents us from trying.

But despite whatever the reason stopping us might be, the fact that we do not get closer to examine the wall or even begin thinking of the possibility of going past it is what keeps us stuck. Because we never stop to think, *Is it really a wall, or am I misunderstanding what it is?*

The biggest mistake we all make is assuming that these "challenges" are really obstacles, or as they might seem to us, walls. This prevents us from seeing them for what they really are, for we are too committed to believing that "This is a wall. I cannot get over it." When we shed this belief, we begin to realize that they are not walls; in fact, there were never any walls.

Anything and everything looks like a wall from far afar. When we get closer to inspect them, we realize that they are actually steps, steps that we can climb to achieve higher heights within ourselves and get closer to unlocking our true potential. When we get closer, we realize just how easy it could be to climb those stairs to keep going forward in our journey once we let go of the "wall" belief.

As you can see from the following diagrams, opportunities, when seen straight on from afar, will look like challenges, like walls. That is why truly attempting to overcome your "challenges" and trying to understand them completely is crucial to fostering growth.

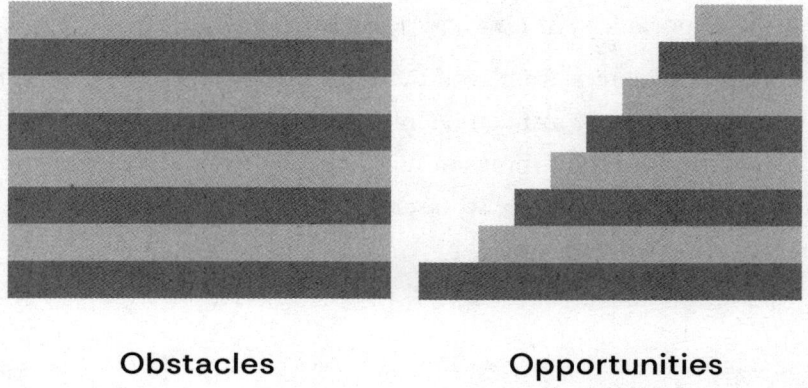

Obstacles   **Opportunities**

But you may ask, "How does this work? How can a challenge be an opportunity?" Well, think of a challenge you faced in your life recently. Maybe you needed to learn to edit videos to create promotional material, or you needed to lead your own team for the first time or learn to use new software to generate a report, or maybe you needed to make a presentation and were uncomfortable speaking in front of others.

If you continue to perceive these tasks as obstacles, you will approach them with disdain, find the quickest way to get them done, and likely cut corners, or avoid them altogether. At the end of the day, you will either quit or be left with zero new skills while producing output that lacks passion and true quality.

If you were to see them as opportunities, however, it might take longer to really understand what you are doing. It might take an extra day to figure out the techniques and create something that you are happy with. But unlike the "obstacle" perspective, regarding every-thing around us as an opportunity leaves us with an improved version of ourselves and allows us to develop the skills to truly do well in areas that are important to us now and possibly in the future.

These challenges are placed there for a reason. Their purpose is to serve you in some form; and almost always, these challenges teach us the most important things in life. Learning from these challenges is what allows those people who seem like they are naturally gifted to excel at everything they do.

Challenges are central to our journeys, and it is up to us to either make them obstacles or opportunities.

There is another way of looking at this very same type of situation. Does life happen *to* you, or does life happen *for* you? This is another mindset that we get to choose.

Recently, my wife, Renee, and I traveled to Australia. We were supposed to fly Air New Zealand from St. Louis to Houston, Auckland,

and Sydney. We had the added stop of Auckland because of flying Air New Zealand, but it was a great fare for the ticket, so we agreed to take that flight.

Our flight from St. Louis to Houston was significantly delayed, so we missed our connection to the international flight to Auckland. This meant that we would have to spend the night in Houston and could not depart until the following evening, effectively costing us a day of our trip.

It would have been really easy to get upset, frustrated, and focused on the things we would not be able to see and do on our lost day in Sydney, but that was not the case. Renee has a cousin in Houston, so we called Les and his wife, Cindy, and they invited us to spend the night at their home. The next day we had a wonderful brunch together, went on a fun hike, and had time to catch up on life as we had not seen them in person in quite some time. It was a marvelous day.

When we went to the airport late that afternoon to take the flight we had been rescheduled on, we boarded a non-stop flight from Houston to Sydney. So after having the bonus time with Cindy and Les, we even had one stop removed from our trip to Australia!

Even if we had not been so fortunate to have a relative or friend in Houston, we could have turned this unfortunate event into an opportunity to experience something fun. We could have found a unique local restaurant to enjoy or possibly taken in a museum that we would otherwise not have had the chance to experience.

It always comes down to our mindset. It is up to us to turn obstacles into opportunities. Every part of life is an opportunity to do something that we might talk about years later, such as the wonderful time we had in Houston.

It is easy to see what is going wrong in any situation, the negative; but when you truly believe that life happens for you, you tend to look for opportunities in any situation. Obstacles become opportunities that become highlights and surprises.

This is the power of a mindset shift. The power that comes with realizing that these very challenges around us are merely opportunities to do what we all want to do deep down—to get better—is unparalleled. This realization will change your life. It will make you embrace your challenges and realize that they are opportunities to grow and flourish. This is the first step toward unleashing your actual potential and building true Momentum in everything you do.

THE "ME" MINDSET VERSUS THE "WE" MINDSET

The second and equally important realization that we need to understand centers on how we perceive life. Is everything we do in life for ourselves? Do I work so I can earn more money, study so I can score better grades, and practice so I can be better at something? When we perceive everything we do in life as intrinsically related only to ourselves, the value we attach to that activity diminishes drastically.

But yet, most of the time, we frame numerous life situations in this inherently selfish manner. We think, *I need to get this work done so I can be satisfied with myself; I need to exercise today to improve my health.* While these activities might, on the surface, seem reasonable to presume as only impacting us, by framing them in this manner we make it much easier for us not to follow through until completion.

The significance of the task is reduced when the only people involved are us being concerned about us.

I can procrastinate my work and skip going to the gym because only I am affected by doing so. More often than not, since we prioritize our immediate satisfaction over our long-term well-being, we are likely to be okay with this sacrifice.

If something matters only to me, then the moment I think, *I will just do this later,* it becomes quite easy to allow myself to drop the commitment. This is because I am not accountable to anyone else, commitments to others are not at stake, and I am not hurting or letting down anyone by not following through on my goals and tasks. I am not even letting myself down, for I have convinced myself that it is okay to do it later.

Most importantly, with a "me" mindset, seeing my goals as purely personal, I will not put in as much effort as I would if I believed they also mattered to someone else's well-being. This is exactly why only having a "me" mindset in every aspect of our lives limits our growth.

How can we switch to a "we" mindset? Moreover, what exactly *is* the "we" mindset? The We mindset is a way of thinking that connects your goals and tasks to people you care about and those around you. It involves realizing that your actions in life affect not just you, nor even just the people in your proximity, but people all around the world.

Nearly everything you do has an impact on someone other than yourself. Realizing this is crucial to understanding the importance and value of your actions. When you begin to connect your goals to the well-being of those around you, the goal's significance increases. With this increase in importance, you become more motivated to follow through on your commitments and push forward on your

Most importantly, with a "me" mindset, seeing my goals as purely personal, I will not put in as much effort as I would if I believed they also mattered to someone else's well-being.

journey. This lays the foundation for achieving true Momentum. It is about realizing that life is also about "we," not always just "me."

Momentum is about realizing that life is also about "we," not always just "me."

This mindset is exactly what set my Purpose and journey in motion. My journey began with me realizing the true value and meaning of accountability and leveraging this powerful idea to transform how people view workplace culture.

What has driven me to pursue and keep pushing forward on this journey is my realization that through doing this, I could positively impact thousands of people worldwide by redefining workplace culture to focus on people and relationships instead of numbers and tasks. This made me deeply value every task I had to do as part of this mission and motivated me to push through any challenge I faced.

My journey was not just about my well-being or satisfaction; it was about spreading this message that I so profoundly believe and value to create a real positive change in other people's lives. This keeps me going to this day and has been crucial for attaining true Momentum.

Think about your life and what you want to achieve. Think about what you want to do and what you might consider to be your Purpose. Once you have done this, take some time to connect this to the well-being of people other than yourself. Understand and realize how this Purpose of yours helps improve the lives of those around you. Switch from a "me" mindset to a "we" mindset, and you will find that it becomes infinitely more exciting to pursue the tasks and responsibilities that are part of this journey.

However, this does not mean that everything you do in life needs to be connected to some larger Purpose that serves someone other than yourself. Personal achievements that only further your own well-being have immense value as well. You might not be able to connect these tasks to a larger Purpose, but these will intrinsically hold value to you.

For example, I have spent weeks training to run numerous marathons for my own satisfaction—I wanted to push myself, achieve something new, and stay healthy. I had no external "we" goal with doing this, but regardless, these marathons held great value to me. Remembering to focus on yourself and taking care of your own well-being is essential to creating the space and energy to focus on goals beyond yourself.

There may not and does not always need to be a broader "we" goal for every personal goal. It is okay to do things for ourselves as well. But more often than not, when it comes to something that relates to our true Purpose, it is often in service to others—for that is intrinsically what tends to drive us forward the best.

Scouting America, formerly known as the Boy Scouts of America, is a youth organization dedicated to nurturing young individuals into becoming responsible, participating citizens and leaders. The highest achievement within Scouting America is becoming an Eagle Scout, which represents a deep commitment to excellence and leadership. It is only achievable through a rigorous and challenging process—only about 6 percent of members have ever earned the Eagle Scout rank.

One of the final requirements of becoming an Eagle Scout is to participate in a service project that benefits someone other than yourself, whether it benefits a community, a school, or even just a few people. This pushes Scouts to dedicate weeks of their time to building something that positively impacts those around them. This also involves finding and motivating other volunteers who are committed to the project. Only after completing this successful Eagle project is it possible to achieve the highly esteemed rank of Eagle Scout.

Why is this project so important to becoming an Eagle Scout—an individual who is recognized for leadership? Certainly, other ways of demonstrating leadership or excellence exist, such as creating a small business or successfully competing in a sport. Yet these are situations where the focus is largely on "me." The success of the business or finishing first in a race are me-focused outcomes. They push me to achieve as much as I need to be personally satisfied.

On the other hand, service and actions to benefit others do something else altogether. It is no longer about how happy I am with my performance, but instead becomes all about how much my actions can benefit and make the lives of others better. In this pursuit, you find that you are constantly driven to be better, do more, and impact

Switch from a "me" mindset to a "we" mindset, and you will find that it becomes infinitely more exciting to pursue the tasks and responsibilities that are part of this journey.

more lives—making a positive impact on someone is so rewarding that it always leaves you wanting to do more. This is what unlocks your true potential and pushes you to be a better version of yourself. This is where Momentum is created.

Thus, to create true Momentum that creates real change in the world, we must start seeing the world from a "we" perspective over a "me" perspective. This prepares us to fully commit ourselves to a larger Purpose and create something we are proud of—something that positively impacts other people's lives.

MOMENTUM AND ACCOUNTABILITY

Momentum and Accountability are inseparably intertwined. Accountability is not simply getting stuff done. That is responsibility. You cannot be held accountable to anything because tasks are simply responsibilities. The sales report is not going to hold you accountable, or as I like to say, "Help you be accountable." You are responsible for *things* and accountable to *people.*

You can only be accountable to people. Accountability is not a way of doing; it is a way of thinking and being. If you are accountable to, and in some situations for, those around you, you will be a reliable and supportive person. You will value people. You will understand, respect, and attend to the needs of others. Your word will be your bond, and you will achieve what you set out to achieve.

And in order to be accountable, you need to be a person who does not make excuses. You need to be someone who pushes yourself and those around you to be the best people they can be.

You are responsible for things and accountable to people.

Well then, do we need to be accountable to achieve Momentum? Or do we need Momentum in the first place to become accountable? The answer is neither and both. They are simultaneous and intertwined. When you become an accountable individual, you will learn to harness Momentum. And if you learn to achieve Momentum, it becomes much easier to stay on top of all your commitments, achieve what you want to achieve, and live an accountable life.

WHAT IS MOMENTUM?

So the question becomes, how do we get into this natural state of *doing* rather than just thinking? How do we unlock our potential and achieve at levels we previously thought ourselves incapable of? How do we move toward our goals with speed, ease, and intention? The answer is Momentum. Momentum is what drives those who excel at everything with ease, who appear to get everything done at the snap of a finger, and who work like they have boundless energy.

But before we delve into what true Momentum is, let us take a look at what the world of Physics says about Momentum.

Scientifically, momentum refers to the speed of an object in motion. The faster the object moves, the higher the momentum. The heavier the moving object is, the higher the momentum. Science multiplies the speed, also known as velocity, and the mass to describe the physical phenomenon of momentum as:

Momentum (p) = Mass (m) * Velocity (v)

"How does this apply to us?" you may ask. Well, much like the just cited formula for the physical concept of momentum, your ability to move toward and achieve your goals and targets with ease and speed can also be broken down into different aspects that come together to form it. To understand what Momentum is, we need to understand what makes up Momentum. Momentum in our lives can be seen as:

Momentum = (Significance * Action) ^{Consistency} – Resistance

Or to make it simpler,

Momentum = $(m * v)^c$ –r

Do not let the formula spook you. Once you understand it, you will realize just how simple and intuitive it is and how powerful it will be for you.

To be accountable, you need to be a person who does not make excuses.

Much like mass in the physics equation, the weight or Significance of what you are trying to achieve is crucial to the Momentum you achieve. If you are trying to work toward something that you do not care so deeply about, you will not feel the energy or focus that comes from Momentum. You will likely be indifferent and try to postpone it till the last minute possible. But if a goal is significant to you and matters deeply to you, Momentum will come much more naturally.

This Significance by itself, however, is not enough to create Momentum. It needs to be coupled with action or effort toward actually trying to achieve the goal. If your action is zero, then no matter how significant your goals are, even if they are multiple bajillions worth of Significance, the outcome will still be nothing, for 0 times 20 bajillion is still zero. When you take action toward achieving your goal, the Significance of the goal combines with your action to create Momentum.

At the same time, if you try to continually work toward something you are not passionate about, then you are likely to experience burnout instead of true Momentum.

So when these two factors of Significance and Action come together, when you work toward something that you are passionate about, the first seeds of Momentum are planted. Working on these activities will inspire you, bring you energy, and drive you to do your best.

However, taking action to achieve this significant goal of yours *once* is not enough. Neither is twice or thrice. You need to consistently and constantly take action to reap the true benefits of Momentum. This is where consistency comes in. If you go to the gym to work on your fitness goals every day for a week and then avoid the gym for months before heading in for another workout session, your results will be very disappointing. However, if you consistently go three times a week, you will start to see huge improvements in your physique. This is because, while Significance and Action matter, they are only truly powered by consistency. Without consistency, your goals are, at best, linear.

True Momentum in your life is not linear. True Momentum, thanks to the power of consistency, is exponential. If you put in twice the amount of effort consistently, you will get much more than twice the better results. That is why the product of Significance and Action is raised to the power of consistency. Because consistency makes your growth exponential. As you pick up speed, more and more positive results start to show up for you. You reach the next level of your endeavors quicker and take on new and even higher goals more confidently. This is Momentum in real life.

However, even though we might do everything we can to achieve Momentum, we might still sometimes struggle. Struggling is normal and natural. It is caused by the numerous excuses, distractions, and fears in our life that might act as barriers against us in our journey to achieve our goals. This is Resistance, and it slows us down.

While sometimes it might be tempting to avoid doing certain things because of the Resistance that we face, such as refraining from starting a new business venture due to the effort and time it requires, the greatest achievements are often hidden behind Resistance. It is in overcoming these barriers that we become the best version of ourselves, and achieve True Momentum.

Momentum is how we get from where we are to where we want to be. Momentum is the secret behind those who seem to achieve everything they want to achieve immediately—the ones who seem to have achieved overnight success. These people are where they are because they have positioned themselves to reap the rewards of Momentum. Though it might seem hard to visually see these people going through this process and easy to convince ourselves that it is virtually impossible for us to get there, that is not the case. There are certain habits and mindsets that allow us to get to where we want to be, and I want to show them to you. I want to show you Momentum.

TWO TYPES OF MOMENTUM

We all strive for two types of Momentum in our lives: Momentum in our activities and Momentum in our life. Without the former, it is impossible to achieve the latter. And so, when you have achieved the latter, the former is naturally already present. But what exactly makes them both different?

Well, think of how many times in life, even when you are brimming with enthusiasm to embark on a new journey to realize your fullest potential, you might often find yourself hindered by what is already on your plate. You may want to learn a new skillset like coding software by taking lessons and practicing consistently every day, but your existing commitment to your current job might make this seemingly impossible.

You might feel like you are already burdened with so many responsibilities from your work that you have no energy or time to begin learning something new. You are thinking, *If I have a hard time getting through my existing obligations, how will I be able to do something new?* This is what stops so many of us from growing, and this is what keeps us stuck in place: *I have too many things to do already.* This is why Momentum within activities is so crucial to achieving Momentum throughout your life.

Momentum within activities is the key to getting everything you need done. This is very important because without sorting out what you are currently responsible for, you will never be able to create the space and energy to pursue what you truly want to pursue. Hence, it is important to learn to develop Momentum within everything you do, whether the smallest task or the most important project of your life. This is the Momentum that will speed up and make the tasks that might seem trivial easier to do. This type of Momentum is what allows you to do the things you *have* to do so that you get to do the things you *want* to do.

Once we have achieved Momentum within the sometimes mundane activities we need to do, we allow ourselves the time and energy to create true Momentum within our lives. This second, fully realized form of Momentum is its most powerful state and what truly has the potential to change your life. But to get there, it is necessary to achieve the first.

Momentum in life is learning to overcome the numerous seen and unseen barriers that prevent us from doing what really matters to us, and creating a real change in the world. This does not mean disregarding important parts of your life such as leisure and family and devoting all of your time chasing your ultimate goal.

To put it simply, *Momentum in activities* revolves around checking off the tasks on our to-do list; it is transactional—while *Momentum in life* gives you the type of energy and focus you need to build an impactful and inspirational business that increases profits year after year, or creates a nonprofit that greatly impacts the community.

These two types of Momentum combine to create True Momentum in your life.

True Momentum will help you achieve unparalleled balance in all areas of your life, ensuring that you succeed in everything you care about, including self-care, relationships, and other impactful goals. Momentum in your life is always connected to a larger Purpose—a Purpose that guides and leads your actions toward something you care about. When carefully studied, this Purpose is always in service to someone else.

True Momentum helps you achieve unparalleled balance in all areas of your life.

Even actions you might pursue to improve yourself are often linked to intrinsically wanting to be better for those around you. By achieving Momentum in your life, you eliminate distractions and barriers and can focus solely with ease on your true Purpose. In the

When you take action toward achieving your goal, the Significance of the goal combines with your action to create Momentum.

pursuit of this Purpose, you create a better reality for yourself and for everyone around you. This is the power of true Momentum.

WHAT DOES MOMENTUM LOOK LIKE?

Momentum is the unseen magic that drives the monumental successes we see all around us. Momentum is the result of invaluable efforts and focus on making the things we really want to happen, happen.

Kevin Systrom and Mike Krieger, two aspiring graduates, spent months building a modest photo-sharing app called Burbn. However, after months of working on the app, they were left with little results and minimal traction. The app was not a success. At this point, many people would have quit. Yet, Systrom and Krieger decided to persevere.

They spent time understanding what needed to be changed to make the app special. They soon realized that the app was too cluttered and decided to focus exclusively on photo-sharing—a simple but engaging feature. After spending much time rebuilding the app and re-launching it, they secured their first few thousand users through word of mouth and simple marketing efforts.

However, soon after as a result of their efforts, Momentum kicked in and led to the app hitting 1 million users just two months post-launch. This rapid increase in users lead to increased investor interest, and ultimately a $1 billion acquisition by Facebook. This is the story of Instagram and it encapsulates the reality of how Momentum can transform efforts into explosive growth.

While this example shows the impact of Momentum and creating something new, how does Momentum look within our careers?

Well, consider the career trajectory of a project manager who joined Google in 2004. He primarily worked on Google Toolbar, a now discontinued feature, before initiating and joining the development of Google Chrome. Over the next decade, he continued to innovate and do what he does best. He pushed himself to take on more responsibilities, eventually overseeing projects like Gmail and Google Maps.

This person put his head down and worked toward all the things he considered significant. He kept putting in the effort and moving forward, until one day, that person became the CEO of Alphabet, Google's parent company. Sundar Pichai is an embodiment of the power of consistent efforts and continuous movement toward one's goal. It is a story of Momentum.

Whitney Wolfe Herd joined the team of the wildly popular dating app, Tinder, in 2012 right before its launch. Being one of the founders of a multibillion dollar company is something that many of us dream of. Yet, when Whitney exited from Tinder in 2014 over alleged harassment, nobody expected her to do what she did next. Most people, when leaving such a prestigious role in a large company, will find themselves feeling depressed and demoralized. So did Whitney. But, she channeled her energy into creating something revolutionary rather than giving up.

The very year of her exit, in 2014, Whitney launched Bumble, an app that required women to make the first move, aiming to change the dynamics of dating and ensure a safer, more respectful environment for women. She channeled all her energy into focused branding efforts, marketing Bumble not just as a dating app but as a movement toward gender equality and a safer dating space.

By the time Bumble went public in February 2021, it had more than 100 million users worldwide. The IPO was historic, making

Whitney Wolfe Herd the youngest female CEO to take a company public in the US.

Whitney's dedication to creating change was what got her onboard as one of the founders at Tinder. And even when she left under unfortunate circumstances, she did not let it faze her spirit and desire to create something big. She kept pushing forward, building on her vision and built her Momentum from scratch all over again, and ultimately ended up achieving immense success.

READING THIS BOOK

I wrote this book as a guide that can help you unlock your true Momentum. As we discovered earlier, achieving Momentum within your activities is crucial to this journey. You need to be able to get your required tasks done so that you can focus on what really matters. But another crucial step in this process is learning to figure out what really matters. You cannot move with Momentum toward something if you do not know what it is that you are aiming for.

So before learning to create Momentum in your life, you must achieve clarity. Moreover, achieving clarity requires you to undergo deep self-reflection on who you are and what you value. I have written this book keeping all of that in mind. I encourage you to read it as a step-by-step guide on building True Momentum, starting with determining what really matters to you and then building Momentum in activities, and finally, Momentum across all areas of your life.

Stop and work through the individual processes as you read. You may very well be surprised by what you discover about yourself.

As I said before, this is my gift to you, and I can't wait for you to see the change that Momentum will make in you.

2

DETERMINING WHAT REALLY MATTERS

Purpose

Mission

Values

Your Purpose is what brings you joy in the service to others.

IT IS QUITE CLEAR THAT MOMENTUM is the key to moving with speed, effortlessly and easily overcoming setbacks. However, where exactly are we moving toward? A ship sailing at speed is meaningless if it does not know where it is going. All you are going to do is get to the wrong place faster.

So then, what is the ultimate destination toward which we are heading? Three key things clarify and strengthen this for us: our Purpose, our Mission, and our Values. I call these the Big Three. The Big Three provide us with clarity, focus, and a true sense of the direction in which we should be moving to build a more accountable life. Each of the three plays a special role in improving our lives and understanding our destinations.

Our Purpose serves as the Why of our lives. Why are we doing the things we do? Why do we push forward and keep going? It is the reason for our actions and pursuits, acting as an internal gyroscope that keeps us moving forward even when the seas get rough. Your Purpose is what brings you joy in the service to others. Your Purpose is unique to you.

Our Mission is the big What?—it defines the goals and objectives we aim to achieve as we journey through life. Our Mission is the tangible manifestation of our Purpose; it is our Purpose in action that guides us in the projects we undertake, the challenges we seek to overcome, and the contributions we strive to make to the world around us. Our Mission may change over time, but new Missions will always connect to our Purpose.

Your Mission is your Purpose in action.

Then come our Values—the "How" of our journey. Think of our Values as a moral compass that ensures that our actions are consistent with our core beliefs and principles. They help align our decisions with our Purpose and Mission, setting standards by which we measure our actions and decisions. Your Values set the standard by which you are known. They ensure that we achieve our objectives in a manner that is true to ourselves and respectful of others.

Your Values set the standard by which you are known.

Which one of the Big Three should we start with? Some people might think that once we figure out What we are doing, it becomes easy to figure out the How and the Why. However, this is a fallacy. The problem with this way of thinking is that it fails to ensure that our decisions align with our true selves, instead opting for a top-down approach. This is not a project. This is your life. Once you know the Why of your life, the What and the How automatically fall into place. Thus, to build from the ground up, it is essential to start with the Why, that is, the Purpose.

PURPOSE
WHAT IS PURPOSE?

Each of us has a Unique Purpose in life. To understand Purpose, we have to start by pondering a question that everyone is bound to have asked themselves at least once in their lives: "Who am I?" Your answer to this question is essentially your unique Purpose in life.

However, this answer needs to be strong and compelling. It must be one that, when you release yourself to it, is no longer a choice but rather your destination. When you embrace your Purpose, a little voice inside you says, "This is who I really am. I have to take action on this. I have no alternative."

Your Purpose provides the direction for your Momentum. Without it, your attention and efforts will likely be scattered, causing you to start and stop projects and weaken your ability to truly achieve Momentum.

When you face something that aligns with your Purpose, it is no longer a question of "Should I?" Instead, it becomes a case of "I have to," much like what my daughter Allison felt when she was out of the car without hesitation to help the injured man. Remember, her exact words were, "I have to go."

How do we find our true Purpose, our "have to"? This intrinsic drive to act upon our Purpose is the essence of Momentum—moving with an unstoppable and magnetic force, drawing others toward us and our Mission.

Often when prompted with this question, many people have told me that their Purpose is to "become rich," "buy a Ferrari," or

True Purpose is focused on people, not things. Purpose is also timeless and unique to us.

"become the CEO of a successful organization." These, however, are not authentic Purposes and are likely a result of confusion about what real Purpose is. If someone assumes that their Purpose is buying a Ferrari, what happens after they do buy the car? They become supposedly "purposeless" or must find a "new" purpose.

Thus, while things such as popularity, cash, or recognition can be goals, they can never be a Purpose. We may need money to survive, and we may need to breathe to live, but neither making money nor breathing is our Purpose. Our Purpose does not end when we achieve a specific goal. Our Purpose is always with us, grounding us and guiding us.

Some people tend to assume that just because they are good at something, it is their Purpose. Simply being skilled in something does not equate to being your true Purpose. Your Purpose might even involve doing something you do not know how to do right now! Purpose is not always, and almost often, outside your comfort zone. It is not necessarily where you are, but rather where you strive to be. Where you "have" to be. Your Purpose is larger than you. It pushes you to become better and greater than who you are right now. It is not something that changes when things around you change; rather, it waits for you patiently, regardless of whether you acknowledge it.

The final, and perhaps most important, indicator of true Purpose is that it is *always* in service to others. This is because, as we discovered earlier, Purpose is focused on people, not things. Therefore, it needs to be focused on aligning with the people you find meaning in serving.

Every human being is born with Purpose, and when you align yourself with yours, you benefit not only yourself but also humanity as a whole. By serving others, we not only fulfill our Purpose but also create a ripple effect of Momentum, inspiring and empowering others to find and pursue their own. This collective Momentum has the power to transform communities and ultimately the world.

No Purpose, no Momentum. Know Purpose, know Momentum.

FINDING PURPOSE

Although it sounds simple, how exactly do we know who we are? How do we understand what our Purpose is, and how do we stop confusing our Purpose with our goals or our job? Before attempting to embark on this journey, I must remind you that it requires time and effort. It is not as simple as identifying what we want in life right now. Instead, it requires you to truly reflect and assess yourself to figure out what your Purpose is.

To help identify your Purpose, answer these questions.

1. Whom Do You Serve?

As our Purpose always connects to the act of service and benefiting humankind as a whole, it helps to consider who you take true joy in serving. This could be teaching people who are eager to learn, serving children who need support, providing value to your company's customers, or even taking care of your family. This service does not feel like a burden. Instead, it feels like you are being your true self, and it becomes a meaningful experience. This service energizes you.

Take a few minutes to write down one or more specific people that you have felt true joy in serving. These are the people who help you recognize your Purpose, and this service is likely to help bring you one step closer to your true Purpose. More importantly, however, try to understand **why** you felt joy in doing what you did.

2. What Is Most Important to You?

Your Purpose needs to connect with something that is significant and meaningful to you. So take some time to consider what is more important to you than anything else. This will give further clarity as to what you really are headed toward in your life.

However, since this is quite a difficult question to tackle in one stretch for nearly everyone, I have broken it down into the following sub-questions that can help bring you closer to a holistic answer:

- What is important to you on a daily basis? What was most important to you yesterday? Why was that important?
- What specific personal goals are most important to you?
- Why are they important now?
- What have you done recently that supports what is important to you? For instance, how does what you did yesterday connect to what is most important to you? Be specific.
- If you own a business: How does your business connect to what you just identified as important?
- Regardless of whether you own a business: Are you looking to get or to give? How do you know? What actions support your answer? WHAT are you looking to give, and to whom?

Write down answers to these questions, even if they are not comprehensive or organized. Just put down your thoughts on paper so that you begin to consider new possibilities and ideas to truly identify what is important to you **in all situations**.

3. Write a Single Sentence Expressing Your Purpose.

It is now time to put together everything you have learned about yourself and comprehensively and concisely express your Purpose. This is your Declaration of Purpose.

Remember to take all the time you need to refine and rewrite your words to distill your most powerful responses into a single sentence. Chances are you will start with something that seems rough or unclear, but through continued thought and editing, you will polish this statement into something meaningful and profound.

Think about what feels good and right for you. Think about what brings you joy. This must be a powerful sentence that speaks the truth **from** your heart and **to** your heart. This is what will keep you going when you doubt yourself.

Write it down and stick it somewhere you will see it often. Let it constantly remind you why you are here and where you have to go. This will be the most powerful single sentence of your entire life.

For example, after spending a long time perfecting it, I arrived at the following as my personal Declaration of Purpose: **To help people discover their potential and be the best they can possibly be**.

Here are some examples from other people who have participated in our Pivot!™ course or have become a Certified Accountability Advisor™ through our certification program:

- My Purpose is to help people and organizations unlock their greater potential in order to amplify the impact they wish to have on those they care about and serve.

- To help people live a life that's in alignment with their values to discover their Purpose.

- My Purpose is to Empower People to Believe in themselves, and their own Potential to DO, BE, HAVE whatever they CHOOSE in Life; and may their Children also grow up with a belief that ANYTHING is Possible.

- To help people discover that they can make a difference and leave a positive impact in the world by improving their relationships and through contribution, with love, generosity, integrity, and faith.

- To help people develop a growth mindset in order to live a purposeful life.

- To inspire people to live the highest vision of themselves in wellness, purpose, and abundance in all aspects of their lives.

- My Purpose is to connect people to their highest good.

- I was placed here to support others in recognizing what is truly important and teaching them to protect it.

- My Purpose is to be a conduit for community and collaboration in both my personal life and career. I want to find ways to inspire others and bring positive vibes to the situations where I can have an impact.

Remember: This is an ongoing process. Years from now, you may still be looking at your Declaration of Purpose and asking yourself, **Have I captured it?** That is the nature of this enterprise. You will become clearer and clearer in your expression of your Purpose the more time you spend "On Purpose."

But do not let that fact keep you from getting as clear as you can be right now about the language that inspires you most. Once you have found that language, reward yourself!

Find some way to celebrate!

ROADBLOCKS TO YOUR PURPOSE

Now that you have identified your Purpose, even after you strongly release yourself to it, it is highly likely that you will encounter roadblocks or obstacles along the way. Although this might seem daunting, this is good news.

It is necessary to encounter Resistance to achieve growth, but it will also serve us well to be prepared for these obstacles beforehand. Remember that those who are at their peaks today did not just get there out of nowhere. They had to climb the mountain, walk through the blizzard, and, like us, struggle to get there.

Vladimir Horowitz, one of the greatest pianists of all time, did not start his illustrious career at the best operas; he spent years practicing and playing in smaller, barely known concert halls across Europe.

It is necessary to encounter Resistance in order to achieve growth.

Jackie Robinson, a world-famous baseball player, did not debut in the major league immediately; he overcame not just racial barriers but also financial hardships of his early life to become one of baseball's greats. Howard Schultz of Starbucks spent years living in public housing before his vision for coffee culture transformed a single Seattle store into a global empire!

Obstacles make us great. It is up to us to make the best of them and perhaps even prepare for them. Some different obstacles we all face in our journeys include:

"If you find a path with no obstacles, it probably doesn't lead anywhere."
—Frank A. Clark

Lack of experience. Most of us are not used to focusing on our Purpose. It takes practice. As kids, none of us could ride a bicycle on our own immediately. We needed some practice, most likely using training wheels to get the hang of it. Over time, however, it became second nature to us. So do not let the lack of experience stop you. Experience comes with time. Until then, remember to be patient with yourself and keep reviewing your Purpose to remind yourself where you are headed.

Holding yourself to an impossibly high standard. Another obstacle is the common mistake of holding ourselves to an impossible standard. Momentum is not about being perfect. It is about being better. Most of the time, there is nothing gained from simply punishing yourself for not being perfect. Instead, it keeps you stuck in your ways for longer. Instead, try to focus on being better. Return to your Purpose, and evaluate what you have done and how you can improve it to move closer to your Purpose. This creates actual improvement, while beating yourself just fosters stagnation.

Excuses. The third and most prominent obstacle that we all face are our excuses. This is the voice inside our head that keeps looking for reasons *not* to take action. Excuses drag us down so much and so often that it is worthwhile examining them in more depth. Usually, we seem to find one excuse that we come back to over and over. I call this our "Big Excuse." It is this Big Excuse that, if we let it, will continually derail our efforts to live our life on Purpose and pursue our Mission. We must face and overcome our Big Excuse if we are to maintain Momentum in our lives. First, we must identify our excuses, and most importantly, our Big Excuse.

Here, for the record, is my big excuse: **"I cannot show my weaknesses."**

Buying into this excuse keeps me from being transparent, inhibits learning from situations, and impedes opening up and connecting with other people and expressing empathy to them. It puts barriers between me, those I could be helping, and those who could be helping me. It keeps me from getting the resources and support I need to improve. When I avoid admitting to myself or someone else that I do not have all the answers, I am buying into my Big Excuse.

Overcoming these roadblocks is not just about facing challenges; it is about maintaining and building Momentum toward achieving your Purpose. Each obstacle encountered and surpassed adds to your resilience and propels you further along your path. Think of Momentum as the force that keeps you moving forward, even when faced with these hurdles. Lack of experience, setting impossibly high standards, and succumbing to our "Big Excuse" might slow you down, but overcoming them accelerates your progress exponentially.

Remember, the key to sustaining Momentum is not to avoid obstacles but to engage with them constructively. By recognizing and addressing each roadblock, you are not just moving past them; you are gaining speed, strength, and determination on your journey toward your Purpose. Embrace each challenge as an essential part of your growth, knowing that every step forward, no matter how small, contributes to building unstoppable Momentum toward realizing your deepest aspirations.

SEEK THE WAVES

An important mindset shift that often goes a long way in redefining your approach to facing challenges is to realize that challenges are not walls. They do not stop you, forcing you to struggle and climb over them. Instead, we can choose to see them as waves. Waves, if you know how to ride them, can propel you forward with Momentum faster than it would be possible by yourself. There is no way more efficient in achieving Momentum than learning to master the technique of seeking out and, eventually, riding the waves.

My wife, Renee, and I are blessed with children who genuinely care about the world they live in and work to contribute at the highest levels. Our eldest daughter, Sara, always wanted to be an attorney. Sara did not just want to be a corporate attorney, going after the largest fees. She wanted to represent people who lacked or had limited access to representation. She knew her Purpose and worked hard to set herself up to achieve it, always staying at the top of her class throughout high school.

Sara was a model student; she took all the honors classes and achieved excellent grades. She was disciplined and passionate about what she was learning. However, she was never truly challenged or forced outside her comfort zone in school to the degree that she could have been. As high school drew to an end, she faced the dilemma of deciding which university to commit to; she was especially torn between two choices. Sara could have attended a very well-ranked university and be part of their very selective honors program, where she would be one of the top-performing students of her class. And being one of the few honors students, she would, by default, stand out.

On the other hand, she had an offer from the University of Pennsylvania, one of the best universities not only in the country but worldwide. Joining UPenn would mean that she would be like every other student in her class: an extremely talented high-achiever. There would be no space to immediately stand out, as everyone was equally academically gifted.

Simply put, she could continue with an environment similar to her high school, where she continues to top the class and stay comfortable. Or she could go to UPenn where she would have to fight and perhaps even struggle to perform well, where the standards were so high that she would have to grow to satisfy them. She could either stay in the shallow waters, or she could wade out into the depths, searching for waves. Sara could have taken the easier road, and sometimes that is fine, but she did not. She chose to ride the wave.

On her first day at UPenn for freshman orientation, she was put on a bus with other students: the people she was going to share her journey with for the next four years. Somewhere along the ride, the minute dust particles floating in the air inside the bus started becoming visible, resembling gold dust, as the sunlight beamed through the windows. Someone decided to point this out, making a remark about how this was caused by the reflection of sunlight on the particles. Another student responded with how this phenomenon was called the Tyndall effect, and soon, the entire bus was filled with discussions over light and refraction, science, and ultimately, passion.

At that moment, Sara realized that she had made the right choice. She was surrounded by people who were so passionate about learning, people who would work hard, challenge themselves, and achieve new heights. And being in this environment would push her to do the same. Sara had jumped on the wave.

During her time at UPenn, Sara met people who would become allies and mentors. She was afforded internship opportunities that were beyond her imagination. Sara even had a summer internship at the Supreme Court of the United States.

The challenges that Sara would face in this new, tougher environment would not keep her from reaching her ultimate goal of becoming an attorney. In fact, the challenges prepared her and positioned her for even greater success. One decision to jump on that wave set

Identify your "Big Excuse" and don't buy into it.

off a cascade of events that would eventually lead her to be admitted to the bar and start her legal career. She had found her next, even bigger, wave.

FINDING YOUR BIG EXCUSE

The most common hurdle that breaks one's Momentum, and in many cases even stops them from starting, are excuses. We *stop* making decisions that align with our Purpose, and instead we *start* making excuses. "There is nothing I can do" is one of the classic excuses—perhaps the most popular one of all. Other persuasive, powerful excuses that take us "Off Purpose" include:

- "I'm too busy right now. I will get to it later."

- "I'm too old."

- "I'm too young."

- "I'm sick."

- "I'm not good enough."

- "This is all I'm qualified to do."

- "I don't have the support to do what is right."

- "It's not the right time."

- "I don't know enough."

- "I don't have the necessary experience."

- "People must (respect me/pay attention to me/ acknowledge me/whatever) before I take action in this situation."

Our excuses also sometimes stem from confusion over what our Purpose is. We must remember not to confuse our Purpose with the supporting activities that come with pursuing that Purpose. Sometimes when I ask a person what their Purpose is, they respond by saying, "My Purpose is to be the highest-paid person in my company."

However, as we discussed, this is a goal, not a Purpose! Their true Purpose might be directly connected to providing the particular service that their company provides. But their false perception of their Purpose might lead to them making excuses such as "At this level, everyone does this kind of thing," or, "If we're going to make our numbers this quarter, we have to look the other way when such-and-such happens, just this once." Do not buy into this way of thinking, for this detracts from your real Purpose!

To truly release ourselves to our Purpose, we must release ourselves from our excuses. Excuses hold us back and prevent us from moving forward and achieving Momentum. We all have numerous excuses for not releasing ourselves to our Purpose, many of them rooted in our early childhood. In my experience, most of us have one big excuse that always seems to materialize when we are about to take action on our Purpose.

It is our job to identify this Big Excuse for what it is—a story that we keep selling ourselves and try to sell to others—and acknowledge it as such. If we never do this, we will keep convincing ourselves that it is a valid reason not to start and not realize it for what it is: an excuse.

You achieve true freedom when you identify your excuses and refuse to be held down by them. This power will help you achieve levels of Momentum that you might have previously thought were impossible. Right now, identify what you feel is your Big Excuse. Write it down. Make a commitment to yourself not to let this excuse get in the way of living your Purpose or Mission.

RELEASING YOURSELF TO YOUR PURPOSE

With your Declaration of Purpose created and your biggest obstacles identified and prepared against, it becomes time to finally release yourself to your true Purpose. When you release yourself to your Purpose, you will feel a true sense of calm within you. You are no longer being pulled in multiple directions and know exactly where you are heading. Decisions become clearer, for you will innately know whether or not you are acting in the service of your Purpose.

That sense of calm is where you are meant to be headed. It is the starting point of any discussion about your Mission, your Values, or your commitments, which means it is the starting point of any discussion about accountability. And certainly, it is the start of creating Momentum. That is why it is so important that you spend the time necessary to figure this out and put it into words that clarify and refine your Purpose.

This sense of direction is also what helps you recognize whether you are truly "On Purpose" or not. When you are "On Purpose" you always feel as though you are grounded, no matter the adversity you may be facing. This is because your Purpose aligns with your true self. When you operate from your Purpose, you are guided by a deep sense of certainty about what you are supposed to be doing, and you are truly effective as you do it. You are focused on what you can control.

Another way of assessing whether you are "On Purpose" is what I call the joy test. Joy is a function of fulfillment, and fulfillment is a sign of Purpose. If your bank account looks good but your fulfillment account, your joy account, looks bleak, you have a problem. You are pursuing goals at the expense of Purpose—things rather than service. Where there is no joy, there is no Purpose. Without joy, Momentum is elusive.

As you commit to your Purpose, every choice and action fuels your Momentum, propelling you forward with increased clarity and effectiveness. The calm and certainty that comes from being "On Purpose" serve as the bedrock for this Momentum, ensuring that you maintain your direction and speed toward fulfilling your goals even in the face of obstacles.

JUST SAY "YET"

Make no mistake about understanding how long it might take you to find your Purpose or to write down your Declaration of Purpose. However, just because it might take you a long time to figure it out does not mean that there is no such "true Purpose" for you. At a deep level, your Purpose is there. You just may not have discovered it—yet. You may not have enough clarity to express and act on that Purpose consistently. But that is about to change.

The minute we say, "I don't have a Purpose," we have done ourselves and the whole human family a disservice. We *do* have a Purpose. Our Purpose is our birthright as human beings. We just need to get better at identifying and acting on it.

So whenever you are confronted with the confusion of not having found your Purpose, just say, "yet." "I have not found my Purpose... yet." Keep working on reflecting within yourself, and it's only a matter of time before it comes to you.

NATURE OF PURPOSE

At any given moment, we are either On Purpose or Off Purpose. Momentum will come when you are On Purpose. When we are Off Purpose, we feel this thing called "stress," and we experience our decisions as difficult. When we are On Purpose, though, decisions are easy. We have a clear sense of direction that makes stress vanish into insignificance and burnout irrelevant.

However, there will be countless moments in our life when we lose our focus and become Off Purpose. This is not something to worry about. This is called being human. The important thing is recognizing when we do this, and working our way back into being On Purpose. This is what your Declaration of Purpose is for! Return to it often. Remember, you can always use it to refocus yourself and put you in the right direction!

Sometimes, however, we might find ourselves in a confusing situation where we do things that feel right but do not exactly align with our Declaration of Purpose. Does that mean we have drifted

Where there is no joy, there is no Purpose. Without joy, Momentum is elusive.

Off Purpose? Not always. It is important to remember that Purpose evolves over time. Much like ourselves, Purpose grows and improves as months and years pass by.

However, this does not mean that our Purpose has fundamentally changed. If we release ourselves to our Purpose and learn to notice our excuses and move past them, then our Purpose will become clearer and clearer to us as time passes and our circumstances change. And something else will happen: we will get better and better at putting our Purpose into words.

But fundamentally, it is always the same Purpose, the same driving force that we recognize in our heart as uniquely ours. Our task is to get better at understanding the heart of our True Purpose, so that we can better fulfill it and put our Momentum into Action.

THE NEXT STEP FORWARD

With your Purpose identified, it is now time to put your Purpose into being, into action, and into reality. This manifestation of Purpose as a tangible force is what creates your Mission. And your Mission is what gives structure to your Momentum. It tells you what exactly you need to achieve, where you need to be, and what you need to focus on to create a true impact. This clarity fuels your Momentum.

MISSION

Your Purpose is the north point on your personal compass. It shows you the direction in which you have to head. However, a compass is not a destination. Neither is my Declaration of Purpose a destination. It is not a place I can actually arrive at in the real world. For me to have that kind of practical destination, I need a Mission that matches up with my Purpose. I need to identify that Mission by asking myself, *What actions support and fulfill my Purpose?*

Your Mission is your Purpose IN ACTION. It is something specific that turns that Purpose into a tangible reality for someone else. It is WHAT you do to take action on your Purpose. Your Mission becomes an integral part of creating and maintaining Momentum.

Your Mission tells you, and anyone else, exactly what it means to step out and go about achieving the Mission. This will provide unmistakable personal clarity about what you are doing in support of your Purpose, the kind of clarity that attracts other people. This type of personal clarity, where your actions are 100 percent in alignment with what you are driven by—when your Why and your What are in sync—makes people naturally drawn to you. That connection is what causes people to sign on to what you are doing. This kind of clarity is an essential prerequisite of true leadership, both within yourself and those around you.

Those who buy into your Mission are your Allies. They might not have the same Purpose, but as long as they support and align with your Mission, they are valuable Allies who will continue to aid you in this journey. To attract strong allies, however, you must have clarity in your Mission and ensure that your actions align with the direction you want to take.

Your Actions Must Always Align with Your Words.

Your Purpose and Mission are intertwined in the deepest manner. Without a Purpose, you cannot have a Mission. You need to understand where you are headed to know how to get somewhere. At the same time, without a Mission, there is no value in having a Purpose. What is the point of knowing that you have to head North, if you are not willing to actually put in the effort to get there?

YOUR MISSION NARRATIVE

Momentum, ultimately, comes from doing. Your Mission is all about *doing*. It is about action that is immediately in sync with your Purpose. Thus, think about what actions you must take to fulfill your Purpose. These will make up the core of your Mission in this world, or, in other words, your **Mission Narrative**.

To build this narrative, you should center it on three action words of your choice. These words should give you and everyone who reads or hears the words a deep and compelling understanding of your Mission. The action words you choose must be unique to you. It is important to notice that these words must connect to your

Your Mission is your Purpose IN ACTION.

Mission Narrative. By extension, these words must also align with your Purpose.

Reminder: As with your Purpose, it often takes much self-reflection and assessment before you arrive at your true Mission Narrative. However, you will know you have found the right Mission when you find that writing or talking about it gives you instant calmness.

This calmness is addictive, and it can exist side by side with profound excitement about your Mission. It is in this calmness that you will build Momentum. This calmness comes from the center of your being, and it appears only when there is total certainty about your Purpose and the action steps you are taking to fulfill that Purpose.

For example, the following is my personal Mission. Notice that it supports and fulfills my Purpose. Notice, too, that I have found three powerful action words to create a Mission Narrative about WHAT I DO that supports my Declaration of Purpose.

This Mission Narrative has resulted in people *worldwide* wanting to be part of and support my Mission—very often, people I do not even know and have never spoken to!

MISSION

My Mission is to build a more accountable world. I serve my Mission through three specific activities:

TEACH

I am a teacher. I educate people on ways to improve and be their best. I share new insights and ways of looking at issues, challenges, and opportunities. I share different ways of believing and thinking.

INSPIRE

Through the use of events, experiences, and evidence I support the beliefs that I teach. This breathes life into the beliefs and helps people take action. I help people awaken to their true Purpose in life.

SUPPORT

I come alongside and help people take the "first step" in their new adventure. I provide ongoing encouragement, tools, and resources to help people stay on course. Change is difficult. We all face challenges throughout our journey. I stay ready to help others overcome those challenges and achieve the goals they aspire to.

My Mission Narrative makes it clear that my aim of creating an accountable world connects to three specific activities: teaching, inspiring, and supporting. It goes into an appropriate amount of detail about what those words mean to me, for the simple reason that what I mean by "teach" may not be the same as what you mean by the word "teach." If I am going to inspire you to support my Mission, it will help us both be clear about exactly what we are talking about. Simply writing down the words Teach, Inspire, and Support does not accomplish that. I must provide context as to what those words mean as I pursue the Mission. In fact, just writing down those words may actually do more harm than good because when people fill in the blanks independently, there will inevitably be disconnects and communication problems.

Your Mission Narrative is extremely important, as it clarifies how you LIVE your Purpose, day in and day out. It is specific and action-oriented, bringing your Purpose into tangible reality. As with your Purpose, while the way you describe it may change, your true Mission will stay fundamentally unchanged over time. True north is still true north. We just get better at recognizing the best pathways available to us. It is on these pathways that we experience Momentum.

LOOKING TO HISTORY

History is full of great people who have centered their lives on unique Missions, prioritizing that in such a way that they have created truly meaningful change in the world. Each of us, I believe, needs to find examples of such people—people whose Mission and whose personal example in pursuing that Mission inspire and motivate us in a personal and powerful way.

Think about the people who inspire you, people who have made a real difference in people's lives, and those whose Missions continue to live on long after their passings. There are thousands of people like that—people whose Mission is so powerful that it outlives them and continues to attract and inspire others.

One such example was the "Happiest Man on Earth," Eddie Jaku. When people call themselves "the happiest," you would expect them to have had wonderful lives filled with joy and comfort. However, Jaku's life was the exact opposite.

As a Jewish teenager during the rise of Nazi Germany, Jaku was forced to face the many horrors of being imprisoned in a concentration camp. Most members of his family, including his parents, were taken away from him and executed in gas chambers. Eddie was sent on a death march, which he narrowly managed to escape, hiding in a forest eating slugs and snails until he was finally rescued.

However, despite all of the destruction and death that he faced every day, after his rescue, Jaku promised himself to smile every day and spread joy. Instead of letting everything he went through beat him down, he decided to find Purpose within his journey. Rather than succumbing to bitterness and hatred, he dedicated the rest of his life to advocating for peace and kindness.

Jaku co-founded the Sydney Jewish Museum in 1992 and volunteered there for decades, giving tours and advice to school groups. Jaku's memoir, published at age 100 and titled *The Happiest Man on Earth*, focuses on the importance of kindness and tolerance and continues to influence and inspire millions of people worldwide.

Through experiencing the very worst, Eddie Jaku found his Purpose in inspiring the very best in mankind, a Purpose he continued to follow till he passed away at age 101. This realization of his Purpose is what allowed him to push past the misery of his early years and become such an icon of compassion and kindness, creating a positive effect on all those around him and inspiring millions more with his story.

While Purpose may sometimes come to you in life-changing situations like Jaku's, it may also come to you naturally without any specific reason at all. As a young girl, born in 1934, she was fascinated with animal behavior and wildlife. She loved using her free time observing native birds and animals and reading books about zoology and biology. She dreamed of spending her time in Africa, observing exotic animals in their natural habitats.

However, she had no prior college education and instead found work as a secretary at Oxford University. Although she could not initially pursue her passions, her desire to go to Africa and study these animals never left her mind. It continued to tug at her heart. Deep down, she knew that it was her Purpose to study and understand the lives of animals. A few years later, after saving up money for her long-anticipated trip, she finally got the chance to visit the country of Kenya, where she had the opportunity to meet a famed anthropologist, Louis Leakey.

Through determination and tenacity, she not only met him but also managed to get hired as his secretary. Leakey, against the objection of many experts, recognized the young lady's drive to interact with and study these animals and sent her on a mission to an island in Victoria Lake to observe the vervet monkey despite her lack of formal scientific education. This sparked a chain reaction, with the lady dedicating decades of her life to studying primates and achieving numerous scientific breakthroughs that have redefined our perception of the relationship between humans and animals.

This young lady also happened to found an institute that has made unparalleled contributions to chimpanzee conservation and awareness all around the world. Today, Dr. Jane Goodall and her institute have become a global force for compassion and a crusader for the ethical treatment of animals. She is a clear example of someone who found her Purpose early in life and dedicated her entire life to not only achieve it, but to continually surpass it, constantly redefining her Purpose to reach greater heights.

Even when doing things that might seem unrelated to her Purpose, such as her stint as a receptionist in Oxford, it can be seen that it was connected to a larger Mission to actually fulfill her Purpose, as this allowed her to save money for her initial visit to Africa.

Dr. Jane Goodall discovered her Purpose as a child and overcame the roadblocks and obstacles she faced because she remained focused on her Purpose. She lived her Purpose fully, making her a true beacon of hope and inspiration.

Your Purpose is always there. It is going to take commitment to discover it and to align your daily activities by identifying your Mission.

"Victory belongs to the most tenacious."
—Roland Garros

At times, you may find your Purpose in your circumstances. A young man who has been inspiring millions worldwide is Chris Nikic. Chris was born in 1999 with Down syndrome, underwent open-heart surgery when he was only five months old, and was unable to walk properly until he was four years old. However, Chris did not let these obstacles become excuses to stop him from achieving big things in life. Instead, he wanted to break the barriers of what it meant to be a person with Down syndrome.

In early 2019, Chris and his dad had an idea of the first barrier they wanted to break: Chris was going to become the first Down syndrome person to complete a full Ironman triathlon. For those who do not know what an Ironman triathlon is, it consists of a 2.4-mile swim, a 112-mile bike ride, and a full 26.2-mile marathon run. It is not a simple task. Chris spent hours every day training and practicing diligently, driven by his Purpose to break the perceived boundaries placed on people with intellectual disabilities. He focused on becoming 1% better daily, trying to run one more lap or do one more sit-up.

In just 11 months since beginning his journey, Chris completed the Ironman Florida, marking a win for all people with intellectual disabilities and earning his place in the history books. However, he did not stop there, for his Purpose did not stop at completing the Ironman. Less than a year later, he completed the Ironman Hawaii, at an even faster time, breaking his own record and making history for the second time in two years.

Today, Chris delivers keynote speeches around the world, and has released his own book documenting his "1% Better" system. He has also become a Global Ambassador for the Special Olympics and has opened the world's eyes to what people with intellectual disabilities are truly capable of. Chris found his Purpose, and despite the challenges presented by his situation, he stuck to it and pushed on, dedicated to living it to the fullest. He is a true inspiration, and I, personally, am excited to see where Chris's Purpose takes him next!

These wonderful people are a testament to the power of Purpose. Their unshakable drive and passion that has led to where they are now is a result of their Purpose and their constant efforts to align themselves with it through their Mission. There are a million more examples out there of people who have done the same. Find your own example! Then become someone like that! Identify your own Purpose and take action on it with an inspiring Mission of your own—a Mission that attracts, instructs, and inspires others!

CRAFTING YOUR MISSION

It is now time to create your own Mission Narrative, similar to how you verbalized your Purpose. Take some time and reflect to write down answers to the following questions, using my Purpose and Mission Narrative as a model to create your own. Think about the Declaration of Purpose you have created as you answer these questions.

Question One:

Whom have you helped joyfully, and what were you doing when you helped them?

Get specific. Take some time. Think of particular people, places, and situations. I recommend taking at least half an hour to jot down particular examples of joyous service in your life.

Question Two:

How do you apply your Purpose right now?

What specific actions do you take that support your stated Purpose? Make a written list of the verbs that capture the DOING aspect of your Purpose from your experiences.

Question Three:

How could you apply your Purpose in the future?

What specific actions do you want to take but have not yet taken that would support your stated Purpose? Make a written list of the verbs that capture the DOING aspect of your Purpose in the future that you most want to live.

Question Four:

What is your Mission?

Draft a single sentence that reflects the ACTION side of your Purpose. This is your Mission. Remember, your Purpose and your Mission are two sides of the same coin. Your Mission is your Purpose in action.

Question Five:

What three activities that connect directly to your Mission bring you the most joy when you think about them?

Review the lists of verbs you have written down and select the three that make you feel the most excited the instant you read them. These three verbs should support your Purpose. Then, write a sentence or two about each that clarifies what that verb means to you in practical terms. Taken together with your Mission, this forms your Mission Narrative.

Now it's your turn to polish your Mission Narrative and share it with your community.

VALUES

With the Why and the What of the journey identified, it is now time to think about the "How." How are you going to get there? How is your journey going to be defined? Your Values embody your principles and your standards of behavior—what is important in your life. They are the *How*. This is the final part of the Big Three that you need to identify to begin the journey of creating Momentum. When you discover and live your Values, you understand exactly how and where to utilize your Momentum.

A Value is something that is extremely important to you. It is so important that if you lost it, you would move heaven and earth looking for it. That is why we call it a Value. You value it.

Your Values are your House Rules. They help you clarify the answers to important questions, such as:

- **What do I believe?**
- **How do I act when no one is looking?**
- **How do we act in this family?**
- **How do we act on this team?**
- **How do we act in this company?**
- **and so on.**

Values determine how we see, connect to, and treat other people. They are the foundation for our relationships with the people in our world. Your Values are timeless. They apply everywhere, all the time. There are no exceptions that can be made with regard to your Values. If they truly are your Values, they will align with your actions every second of your life. And every action that aligns with your Values propels you forward with integrity and drive, accelerating your Momentum toward achieving your goals.

Yes, there are going to be times when you slip up. You are human. However, it is important to understand the two different ways people tend to slip up regarding Values. If you inadvertently make a decision that does not align with your Values, you need to notice it, acknowledge what happened, and fix it fast.

However, if you have a pattern of making a decision that purposely violates a stated core Value—meaning you know full well that a given decision will violate the core Value you say you have, and you consistently make that decision anyway—then you do not have that Value. You are not living it, period.

Our Values are only ours if we truly commit to living them. If we don't, then we become liars. Saying we value something when our actions do not support that value is just a lie. And if we continue lying to ourselves in that fashion, we will never truly become purposeful, and true Momentum will always be outside our reach.

WHY LIES ABOUT VALUES HAPPEN

Usually, people lie about their Values because they follow the common pattern of (publicly) adopting a certain Value without considering whether the Value in question is truly important to them. The Value that comes out of their mouth is not what they believe. Remember: A Value is something that is so important to you that you move heaven and earth to restore it if you happen to lose it.

Sometimes, people start talking about a given Value because they think doing so makes them look good, or because they think it is what a particular individual wants to hear, or because some other person or organization publicly adopted the Value and they want to be like that person or organization. This kind of Value is pasted on from the outside. It has nothing to do with the individual proclaiming it. It is what the person thinks is supposed to be important, not what actually is important.

Never select a Value to live by because you think you are supposed to. Select a Value to live by because it is important to you personally—because it is true to who you are, it is what you believe, it is rooted in truth, it respects the rights of others, and it is what you are willing to honor in your actions and choices.

THE NATURE OF VALUES

Values come with a peculiar characteristic: only you truly know whether you are living them or not. You can convince others and sometimes yourself that you are truly living your Values. However, for them to truly be effective, you need to constantly evaluate every action of yours to ensure that they really do embody your Values. My point is, talk is cheap. If all you have is talk, and there is nothing that aligns with any commitment you make in support of your core Values, and talk is all that happens, then you are not really living your Values.

Someone who is not manifesting their Values in action is someone who is lost as to who they really are. Such a person does not have a clear idea of themselves and, thus, is less likely to have clarity about where they are headed, barely possessing any form of Momentum in their lives.

Words about what we value are meaningless without action. It is up to each of us to define what our Values mean and then to live up to what we have defined. A clear set of Values must look you in the eyes at the moment of decision, the moment you are tempted to take a course of action that is contrary to who you really are and tell you, in a way that stops you cold, "You are better than this."

So remember this: Your Values are yours. They are not designed to make you look good in front of others. Your Values must come from a place of Integrity. You must live your Values even when no one is watching you.

SELECTING YOUR VALUES

Your Values are what make you tick. When you figure out what is most important to you, you figure out your Values.

As with your Purpose and Missions, selecting your Values requires a lot of self-reflection. To aid this process, answer the following six questions to gain a deeper understanding of yourself.

I have taught this system for a long time with people from around the world, and without fail everyone experiences amazing results. Step through these questions and experience this incredible journey for yourself.

Question One:

Who are your heroes?

On a separate sheet of paper, I want you to write down the names of five of your Heroes. These should be people who have inspired you and made you think, *Hey, I really want to be like that person.* You may have known them personally; you may not have. The people on your list could be living or dead. They could be fictional or real. All that matters is that the person is someone you admire deeply, someone whose example has made a difference for you and who has emerged as a role model.

So, for example, you might list the following people:

Abraham Lincoln

My grandfather

Spider-Man's Uncle Ben

Marie Curie

Martin Luther King Jr.

Question Two:

Why are those people your heroes?

Next to each of those names you just listed, I want you to write at least five words or brief phrases that describe specific personal qualities or traits that made you choose that person for your list. So, for instance, if Lincoln was one of your Heroes and you were personally inspired by his quote, *"I am not bound to win, but I am bound to be true; I am not bound to succeed, but I am bound to live up to what light*

I have," then you might lead your list with the word Integrity. Your full list for Lincoln might look like this:

Abraham Lincoln:

Integrity

Committed to his cause

Eloquent

Kept his Purpose in focus no matter what

Strong in adversity

Wise

Saw the Big Picture

Do this for all five names on your list. Again, notice that even though you never knew Lincoln personally or never could know Spider-Man's Uncle Ben in real life, you *can* identify the ways of acting, thinking, communicating, and making decisions they displayed that have had a positive impact on you—their traits that have made you think, *I want to be like that.* The words you list for each figure should answer the question: *Why them?*

When you finish Question Two, you should have at least *twenty-five* qualities listed—at least five for each person you have chosen.

Question Three:

Where are you right now in relation to your Heroes' qualities?

For *each* of the qualities you have listed, I want you to honestly state where you are right now in your life with regard to living that quality on a scale of one to ten. Be tough on yourself here. The only person who will read this sheet is *you*. Give yourself an accurate assessment in each area. Understand that a score of 10/10 means you never deviate from the highest standard set by your Hero in that area.

Ask yourself, in every area where you do not give yourself a 10 out of 10, why you gave yourself the score you did and what you would need to do to reach a score of 10 out of 10. (This part of the exercise can be the focus of a later discussion you have with your Accountability Partners.)

Once you have done that, I want you to underline the *one* quality for each Hero that you *most* wish you had in your life.

Your list for Lincoln might now look like this:

Abraham Lincoln:

<u>Integrity</u> (7/10)

Committed to his cause (6/10)

Eloquent (7/10)

Kept his Purpose in focus no matter what (8/10)

Strong in adversity (6/10)

Wise (6/10)

Saw the Big Picture (6/10)

Question Four:

What are the five qualities you have underlined?

Review your long list and use it to create a shorter list of *five* underlined traits or qualities, one from each person you've chosen as a Hero.

Your list should now look something like this:

Abraham Lincoln: Integrity

My grandfather: Respect

Spider-Man's Uncle Ben: Contribution

Marie Curie: Self-Improvement

Martin Luther King Jr.: Significance

Congratulations. You have just created a first-draft list of your core Values. That is a start. But it is not the end!

Question Five:

What does the second draft of your list look like?

Using your first-draft list, your next job is to check how well it matches up with the following four Value Categories and revise it so that it fulfills all four. You may need to go back and use words you developed earlier in the process to do this.

> **Which words on your list are <u>foundational</u> Values? Foundational Values are the basis or framework on which everything else stands. They identify the one thing you will never, ever compromise. (For Lincoln, that Value was Integrity.) Foundational Values speak to your character.**

Which words on your list are <u>relational</u> Values? These Values affect the way in which two or more people behave toward and deal with each other. Notice that Integrity can be expressed as both a foundational Value and a relational Value.

Which words on your list are <u>professional</u> Values? Note that you can and do have professional Values, whether or not you have a job. These Values affect the level of quality and excellence with which you approach any undertaking. Your professional Values determine the level of quality and excellence you deliver, regardless of what you happen to be doing or whether you are being paid to do that. Note that Integrity, Self-Improvement, and Significance—meaning the desire to create meaning and inspire others to be, do, and achieve their full potential—can all be expressed as professional Values.

Which words on your list are <u>community</u> Values? These Values affect how you feel about, participate in, and support your community. Note that Contribution can be expressed as a community Value and also as a relational Value governing your interactions with others—or both.

This part is important: **A great list of core Values ticks all four of these boxes.** Revise your list until it does. This may mean tweaking the number of core Values on your list. There is no right number of core Values, although I will say that if your list contains more than seven, it may be unwieldy and hard to remember. Do your best to narrow the focus while retaining the meaning and Significance.

When your list ticks all four boxes, you will have a viable second draft of your list of core Values. But that is not the end of the process!

Question Six:

What is the narrative for each of your core Values?

Just writing down a list of words is not enough to establish your core Values—not by a long shot. For one thing, each word you have chosen needs to be clearly defined so that it is obvious what unique meaning it carries for *you*. What you mean by Integrity may be very different from what someone else means. Not only that, but the meanings of your core Values are likely to become clearer to you over time. You need a Narrative.

In this context, a Narrative is a written statement of what you DO to ensure that the Values show up in your world. The Narrative helps you get the key distinctions down on paper so that you can review them a month, a year, or a decade from now and make whatever changes are necessary in light of your overall life experience and any new perspectives you've gained over time.

In writing the Narrative and gaining clarity about what each Value means to you, you will also gain deeper insights into which Values fall into which of the four categories I have shared with you: foundational, relational, professional, and community. Remember, one Value can attach to one, several, or all four of the categories.

Here again, for illustration purposes, the following is the Narrative that supports my Values. Use it to get a clear sense of what a Narrative looks like. *Do not* use it as something you can cut and paste into a file and pretend it is your Narrative. *Do* use it as a model for bringing your own core Values to life.

INTEGRITY

I make decisions based on the belief that my word is my bond and doing what is right is always the right thing to do. I commit to this no matter what.

RESPECT

I see all people as equal. I value other people's opinions, appreciate their beliefs, and recognize the importance of their priorities.

SIGNIFICANCE

I create meaning in my life and the lives of the people around me. I look for ways to create significance for my family. I make the effort to get to know people. I look for potential in the people with whom I come in contact. I encourage people. I participate in my community and work to make a difference.

Life is an adventure. I actively live that adventure when I live with integrity, respect, and significance.

"Be strong and resolute."

Remember: *Only when your actions align with your core Values are the Values yours.* If you look back at the end of the day and find you made *no* decisions that align with your core Values, you need to fix something. Values are not to achieve at some point in the future. They are right now.

Write your Core Value Narrative in your own words. Do not use my Narrative or anyone else's verbatim. Identifying and committing to your Values is a continuous process. To keep improving your alignment with these unshakable Values, always ask yourself for each of your core Values, *How is this NOT showing up in my life—and where could it be showing up more?*

THE IMPACT OF VALUES

The greatest ideas are often born from a conscious effort to live our values. Jenny Nguyen has a deep love for women's sports. In 2018, having to plead with a bartender to watch a women's championship game on one of the smallest TVs at a mostly empty bar left her extremely upset.

What bothered her most was not that she had to struggle so much just to watch women's sports on an otherwise unused TV; instead, it was how she was used to having to do so. This had become the norm for Jenny, her friends, and others who enjoyed women's sports. Even if no major men's games were going on, they had to struggle to watch women's sports in such social spaces.

Jenny realized that it was not just about disregarding women's sports but rather about the lack of inclusion. The reality that even extremely high-stakes and thrilling women's championship games were disregarded for no practical reason struck her hard. It reflected the lack of inclusivity toward women that characterized traditional sports bars.

Jenny began thinking of possible solutions, eventually coming up with the idea of a women's sports-only bar. As a joke, Jenny called her imaginary bar "The Sports Bra." This joke stuck around in her head for years, nagging at her mind as something she could potentially do to make a positive change in the lives of both herself and those around her.

After years of thinking about it, Jenny finally decided to take action. She felt that if she could get even one child to feel like they belonged in sports, her idea would be worth it. Jenny wanted to create a place of inclusivity and empowerment for those who felt as if they did not belong anywhere else.

Jenny was not alone, people worldwide wanted this change: they wanted a place where women could enjoy women's sports and feel included while doing so. So, they supported it. All they needed was someone actually willing to act on it.

Today, The Sports Bra is a huge success. Multiple women's sports stars, including former professional basketball players Sue Bird and Diana Taurasi, have visited the bar for sponsored events. The bar is always packed full of energy, with only one thing playing on TV: women's sports.

The secret to the incredible success of The Sports Bra is not just its innovative business idea, good ambiance, and effective marketing. Jenny's vision succeeded because it connected to her values, which were felt and connected with by so many other people. The secret to any successful venture is its foundational values. Jenny built her bar with a mission to create an inclusive place where people feel like they belong, and that connected with all those who wanted a place to belong.

Jenny is now in action to open franchises across the United States. Jenny has expressed that she wants the people she grows with to have similar values.

People connect through values. We very rarely, if ever, connect through products and services. Strong, positive values attract strong, positive people. Building communities of people who align with a set of values, be it an organization or simply a social network, creates powerful groups of people who can and will accomplish great things.

The journey becomes inevitable when you begin to move toward something you value and make it your Purpose. It no longer is a choice, you just have to do it, for it calls out to you. Jenny found her calling and dedicated her efforts and time to it. Before she knew it, Momentum took over and helped her reach heights she had not dreamed of. All she had to do was discover what meant something to her on a deep level that aligned with her values and start working toward it. And today, she inspires thousands of people worldwide to do the same.

At the same time, companies often boast about having numerous core values, such as excellence, integrity, and innovation, which seem overused and cliche. They may state these values but are they living them?

Another company that is truly built upon and makes every decision revolving around their values is Bombas, a sock brand built upon giving. The company's unique proposition is that for every clothing item purchased, an item of the same kind is donated to homeless shelters. You buy a pair of socks, they give a pair of socks. Every purchase leads to a positive change in the world.

Bombas was created in 2013 when its founders, David Heath and Randy Goldberg, discovered that socks were the #1 most requested clothing item at homeless shelters. The brand was founded upon the value of giving and stayed true to it even during turbulent times like the Covid period. Heath recalls how while other companies were

People connect through values.

trying to boost business during the pandemic, Bombas was working to help the people most affected by the lockdown—the homeless.

Staying true to their values not only allowed them to make a positive change but also boosted sales by as much as 40 percent as people recognized the brand's commitment to giving. Through buying from Bombas, customers indirectly helped other people in need also.

Moreover, Bombas has grown its network to more than 3,500+ partners in the United States who share their values. This enables them to build an intricate and robust network with thousands of homeless shelters across the country. Through partnering with other companies who share similar values, like Cleancut and Brooklinen, Bombas can collaboratively drive an even deeper positive change.

In its first 10 years, Bombas created an astounding brand with a net worth of $550 million, not just because of its high-quality products, but because of the strong relationship it has built with its employees, customers, and other companies as a result of its persevering commitment to its values.

THE NEXT STEP FORWARD

Growth is not a one-off event. It is persistent, ever-present, and continual. The true benefit of everything discussed so far is realized when you make understanding and living your Purpose, Mission, and Values an everyday process.

Take two minutes each morning just to think about your Purpose, Mission, and Values, and how they match up with your decisions. Take one value and think about how it did or did not show

You must know where you want to go to move forward with speed and ease.

up yesterday. Now, think about how to incorporate that value into everything you do today. This is essential to achieving Momentum in your life. You must know where you want to go to move forward with speed and ease.

What powers this journey:

- **The Why:** Why do you want to go there? This is your Purpose.

- **The What:** What are you going to do to get there? This is your Mission.

- **The How:** How are you going to get there? This is living your Values.

The answers to these questions are fundamentally set in stone. However, this does not mean they do not evolve and grow over time. The further they grow, the clearer they become. And the clearer they are, the easier it will be to achieve true Momentum.

When these three forces come together, you create an environment where Momentum can be fostered. This is what powered and gave Allison the energy and focus to instantly leap from the car and stand in a pool of gasoline for an hour to help the injured man. Allison did not have to stop to think about it. It was a moment where her Purpose, Mission, and Values perfectly aligned with her actions, and that gave her the Momentum that fueled her.

When we understand our Purpose, Mission, and Values, and start to live them, we take the essential first step toward setting ourselves up to harness the power of Momentum. Now, let's take a look at exactly how we bring Momentum into being. Let's discover the system, and exactly what we need to do to make this happen.

3

DISCOVERING AN IMPLEMENTATION SYSTEM

WITHOUT TAKING ACTION, Momentum can never be achieved. And that is exactly why starting is so crucial, for once we take the first step, the first action, it essentially compounds and fuels our Momentum.

Thus, it is time to commit to a system that will help us take action—a system that will simply help us start and complete what we need and want to get done. Understanding the natural barriers to starting any task is important, but it is more important to be able to take that next step and move forward.

What if something as simple as snapping your fingers could change your life? What if you could snap your fingers and set all those tasks on your to-do list in motion? What if you could snap your fingers and get it all done? Well, you can. Let me explain.

As we have seen, the hardest thing to do is to start. It is the physical and mental act of making the effort to begin doing the task that is in front of us. Often, we find ourselves unable to start due to various reasons that vary with each goal we pursue.

For an assignment that is due in two weeks, you might find it tempting to procrastinate, for the luxury of time makes it easier to push it off. And more often than not, it is only when this cushion disappears that we face the stone-cold reality that it is no longer due in two weeks but instead is due tomorrow. So, we panic and start working on it.

Sometimes, you convince yourself there are other pressing things to attend to, using that as a reason not to start working on your goals. "I need to do my daily tasks, so I will not have enough time to start writing that weekly newsletter that I have been wanting to release." Excuses and reasons come in all forms and types because different tasks, goals, and projects come in different shapes and sizes, requiring different energy, involvement, and care.

To successfully get started, with Momentum propelling you forward, you must first understand what kind of goal is in front of you and what it needs from you. Remember, I asked, "What if you could snap your fingers and get it all done?" Well, that is exactly what I want to teach you how to do. Every goal or task you have can be evaluated on four fundamental questions:

1. Is it **Significant?**

2. Is it **Necessary?**

3. Is it **Achievable?**

4. Is it **Priority?**

Considering these questions helps us understand what might be holding us back from starting on that goal, task, or project and how to build the Momentum that harmonizes well with it. This is the SNAP framework. Let's look at the four aspects of SNAP in more detail.

A *significant* project is important to you. One that is meaningful enough that you really look forward to doing it rather than simply getting it done. This could be finally launching that new product you have been planning for months, starting an initiative to help those in need within your community, or even finally starting your personal blog. These projects are significant to you as a person and can make a difference to those around you. These are the projects that make you feel good as you are working toward them. These projects impact not just you; they also impact others on a meaningful level.

A project's *necessity* is often supplied through an external force, such as a supervisor or a deadline, pushing you to get something done. The performance reports that you must turn in every Friday or

What we believe matters.

the daily homework you need to complete. Necessary projects cannot be perpetually delayed or pushed, as you are often held responsible for completing them. However, these might also be projects that get pushed until the very last minute.

Whether a project is *achievable* or not often comes down to three different parameters: time, feasibility, and belief. Mostly, it is the former, where although you are confident that you can achieve the project, it may be impossible in the given time period. A competitive job application requiring numerous long-form responses is unachievable if you only discover it 30 minutes before it is due. There simply is insufficient time to craft these responses before the application closes, making them unachievable due to time.

On the other hand, certain projects, such as writing an academic paper, might be unachievable as they are simply not feasible for you if you do not have sufficient research experience or guidance. However, what might not be feasible today will not always be so. Given time and effort, these projects might very well become easily achievable later down the line. You may not be able to run a marathon today, but if you train carefully and over a sufficient amount of time, you may very well be able to complete the race.

And sometimes, while we may think something is not achievable, we might simply be wrong. Sometimes, we do not really know what we are capable of. Sometimes, the people around us can better see our capabilities. Alternatively, while others may think we are incapable, we may believe we are, and through persistence, we achieve our goal. What we believe matters.

Last, the question of whether something is a *priority* often boils down to time constraints. Given everything you have on your plate right now, what should you attend to first? This could be prioritizing one project over others due to its importance to your career or choosing to devote more attention to a certain assignment as its deadline is closer. At the same time, priority could also translate to postponing a meeting to attend your child's dance recital.

Unlike necessity, priority is not just mandated by external influences but something that you can also set internally. Your values, such as attending your child's dance recital, may dictate your priorities. If you value family, you will find a way to prioritize it. However, that does not mean you will neglect other important tasks and projects. Prioritization is the art of figuring out how to satisfy all of your commitments and live all of your values. You have to live all your values, support all your relationships, and fulfill all your needs. This can be challenging, but it is a responsibility that we all carry.

The items on your to-do list will all fall into one of the regions of this diagram. There are specific reasons why we struggle to start any specific task. And there is a simple way to overcome that reluctance to start and finish a task. Understanding this is imperative to starting, and without starting, it becomes impossible to attain Momentum.

In the following diagram, each circle represents one of the four aspects: Significant, Necessary, Achievable, and Priority. Let's examine some of these regions, consider what may be holding you back, and consider how to overcome those challenges.

SNAP

The closer your goal, task, or project falls to the center of the diagram, to the area marked as 4, the easier it will be to start. Thus, it is essential to understand where the task currently lies and why that makes it harder for you to start. The more we understand why we

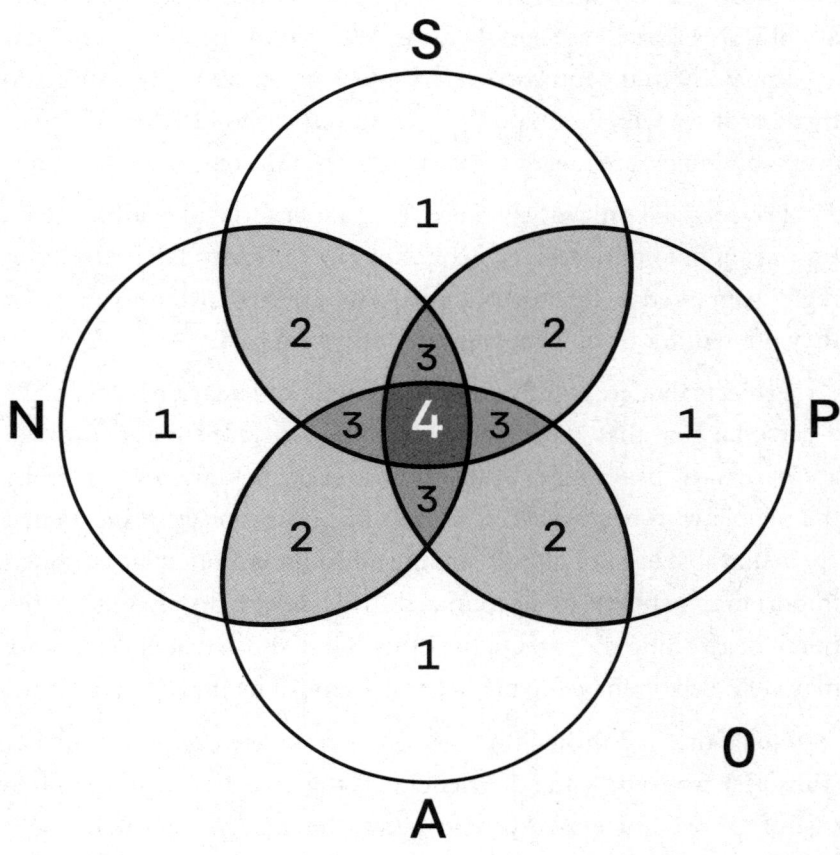

are struggling to begin a particular task, the better we can evaluate the situation and how we actually accomplish what we really need to accomplish.

Many projects in life are neither significant, necessary, achievable, or a priority at the moment. Ultimately, these tasks that fall outside all four SNAP areas are simply ideas. We should consider them later at some point in the future to determine whether we really want to do them or if we will eliminate them from our to-do list. Not all ideas, even good ones, are meant for us actually to take on.

Projects that only satisfy one of the four criteria, like ones that are significant but not necessary, achievable, or a priority, fall in the outer regions, marked as Region 1. These goals are the hardest to start, for they often differ from what you currently want to do.

Projects that are significant to you might often lack necessity, like a personal goal that keeps being pushed for lack of time. Those that are necessary, like a report due at the end of the day, are wanted by the people who necessitate it, such as our boss, not us. Projects that are achievable are not always significant to us and often lack enough importance actually to be pursued. This might be repainting the porch or cleaning the car. On the other hand, those that are a priority may very well often be too big of a task to finish by the preferred time.

Goals that fall in Region 2 are often relatively easier to start but still suffer from the same deficiencies as the earlier case. In the same case of a short film, even if you possessed the skills to make it, it would still be quite difficult for you to get started on it if it was not necessary and not a priority in your already packed schedule.

However, most goals you will likely actively pursue fall within Region 3. They satisfy most of the criteria to be something you can quickly get started on but do not satisfy all four. There are four different types of such projects. Consider projects that are "SNA," or in other words, significant, necessary, and achievable but not a priority given your current situation.

This might be you going to the gym regularly. You really care about your fitness; it is necessary to keep you healthy, and you have an hour of free time in the evening on most days. However, you also have a rapidly approaching deadline for a major project on the horizon, and thus, do not consider exercise a priority, making it very difficult for you to start.

Projects classified as SNP might be the exact projects you are worried about. You deeply care about the project's outcome; it is imperative for you to perform well, and it is your key priority right now. Yet, you also manage your company's daily social media posts, which are mandatory to maintain its brand presence, and this takes up a large part of your day.

Thus, given your current commitments, you feel completing the additional project on time is impossible. And if you believe something is impossible, you feel there is no point in wasting your time trying to accomplish it, preventing you from starting on it.

SAP projects are commitments in life that you likely keep pushing off because you do not think they are "necessary," like the long overdue vacation after stressful work periods. The vacation is significant to you, achievable, and a priority to reduce stress and replenish your energy.

However, you do not consider it immediately necessary, instead pushing it off for "later," as without it being explicitly mandated as a need, you find it hard to justify. Thus, you perpetually delay that one vacation that should have happened years ago.

Last, and likely populating your to-do list, are the NAP projects. These tasks make you wish you were NAPping instead (pun intended), like your repetitive reports that must be turned in to your supervisor every Monday, homework assignments, or cleaning your car. These are necessary priorities yet insignificant and unimportant to you personally.

Any excuse to delay or not start these tasks that possess barely any gratification or meaning to you is utilized. Consequently, these goals get pushed until the very last minute, or the deadline, before they are half-heartedly done.

However, despite the different reasons making it hard to start each task, one factor is shared across all. They all revolve around a fundamental part of the Momentum equation presented earlier—Action. Recall the formula for Momentum:

$$Momentum = (Significance * Action)^{Consistency} - Resistance$$

This is important; remember, the easiest thing to do is to do nothing, and the hardest thing to do is to start. While an NAP task might require a different approach from an SNA task to ensure that you do not give up immediately after starting, they are united in the fact that regardless of their type, you need to start. Nothing happens until you begin.

ALL IT TAKES IS SNAPPING YOUR FINGERS

Before tackling the challenge of successfully persevering in our commitment to achieving these various types of goals, how do we even begin? What is the key to actually starting?

While writing this book, I conversed with someone on my team, Arjun. I said that I want people to finally just get done what they know they need to achieve. I want it to be easy for them. I want them to be able to achieve immediate action. Arjun said we need a trigger—and he inadvertently snapped his fingers. That's when it hit me. If we commit to something as simple as snapping our fingers, we can better commit to completing the tasks we know we need to do. And we can get them done now.

If we commit to something as simple as snapping our fingers, we can better commit to completing the tasks we know we need to do.

The easiest thing to do is to do nothing, and the hardest thing to do is to start.

As with many things in life, it is simply a commitment to ourselves. One snap of our fingers, and we start. We must critically reflect on what lies ahead of us and connect the goal to the SNAP framework we have learned. If a goal is significant, necessary, achievable, and also a priority, or even if it satisfies a few of the four criteria, then it may be worthy of a snap, a snap of our fingers. We all have many tasks and projects that only satisfy one or two of the SNAP criteria, but we must do them.

This, however, is not an imperative to pursue each and every project that we come across. At times, we might have projects that might be Significant or Achievable, but the timing might just not be right. If a project, goal, or task meets the criteria, we consider it. But it does not mean we must always say *yes* to it.

Sometimes, we are defined by what we say *no* to. This framework is essential to understanding the things that do not deserve our time or energy.

If you would not snap to start a task, then it is not worthwhile pursuing. It is important not to waste your time in pursuit of these tasks, for it is essential to keep your plate free and time available to focus and dedicate your energy to the things that really matter to you, your well-being, and the people around you.

We all have a basket of things that we must do, whether we want to or not. The SNAP criteria help us figure out what falls in our basket and what falls outside—it channels our focus and energy to what really deserves it. SNAP helps us prioritize with meaning rather than simply procrastinate indiscriminately.

We must commit ourselves to the SNAP. I only snap my fingers when I believe in the importance of completing this task; when I snap, I commit to starting. Snap to start. No matter how large or small the task.

This may sound simple, but you will be amazed at your results once you commit. Look at your list of tasks. Everything you are considering must meet at least one of the four criteria. Then, pick which one you need to get done next. Snap your fingers.

Yes, I know this may sound silly, and who knows what the person in the cubicle next to you might be thinking when you snap your fingers, but who cares? You are about to become super productive. You are going to create Momentum. Here is the key. When I snap my fingers, I commit to taking the first step toward the task I'm considering. I define a commitment as "No Matter What!" So, yes, I *have* to start.

Once I start something, it is much easier to stick with it and finish it. The act of snapping my fingers ignites something inside me that helps me get going. This initiates Momentum. Momentum takes over at this point, and I work to finish the task. Then I pick the next task, snap my fingers, and fulfill my commitment by starting that task.

I need to proofread an article, so I snap my fingers and get it done. I promise to send a video to a client by tomorrow, so I snap my fingers and turn on the camera to begin recording. I need to connect with a friend, so I snap my fingers and dial his number.

It is simple, but it is not always easy. We need to remember that, as children, many of us could not snap our fingers. We might mimic the action, but the audible snap would never come. But instead of letting this stop us, we continue trying again and again until finally, we hear "SNAP." And once we master it, it becomes natural to do it at any time we please.

The same applies to using the SNAP principle. The key is your commitment to the SNAP principle, which I am asking you to make. Commit to the SNAP and stick to the physical activity of snapping your fingers as a trigger to start your work, and it will become cemented in your mind before you know it. Snap your fingers before you start every task that lies before you.

As you keep doing this, your mind and spirit become attuned to the act of snapping to start. It becomes natural. It becomes our push to start, for we recognize the Significance, priority, achievability, or necessity of the project ahead of us. We may not want to do something, but we know we need to, so we simply snap our fingers and take the first logical step.

Snap to start!

This does not mean that you simply snap for any and every goal. For a snap to be effective, it must be connected and utilized for a task that satisfies the SNAP criteria we discussed. Unless a task is significant, achievable, a priority, or simply a necessity in some form, it will not be possible for you to start. And, if it is a project that you do start, you probably will not finish it. We've all been there!

A snap is only effective when the task is worthy of it. This is why you must reflect and understand the task and its importance before starting. It is important to identify and understand which tasks are not worthy of a snap, for these are not worth your time either.

Snap to start. No matter how large or small the task.

Some tasks are more difficult to commit to than others.

I use SNAP to take on and eliminate all those mundane things that need to be done. I want to get them out of the way to get to those items that carry more Significance. Completing these unexciting tasks is what gives me the time and energy to focus on more meaningful projects. This sets me up for Momentum. This is where I know I will be able to focus on projects that have a greater impact and contribution to the people around me and my community.

Sometimes, you have to do what you have to do, so you get to do what you want to do.

I find that the most difficult tasks are those that are only Significant. Let's say you want to start a food bank in a community to support families who do not have enough food. This is a fantastic idea. It is powerful. You will feel great achieving it, but more importantly, you will profoundly impact many people's lives.

On the surface, it may not meet the criteria of Necessary, Achievable, or Priority. It is important in your heart, but the timing is such that it will not happen now for various reasons. So we do not just look at this project and snap our fingers.

At some point, we all have to look in the mirror and ask ourselves if we are really serious about doing what we think we should be doing. In this case, we ask, "Am I really going to spearhead establishing that food bank?" Here is what I know—change is just a decision. Once we decide to do something and commit to "go," the solutions to problems and answers to questions will naturally present themselves.

If you decide to commit to that food bank, you will figure out how to get it done. Once you snap your fingers, you will move heaven and earth to make it happen because of its Significance to you and its impact on others. Although these types of projects may be difficult to start, once you do, you will be amazed at what you can achieve.

So, the bottom line is that as long as we can satisfy at least one of the four areas—Significant, Necessary, Achievable, and Priority—we know the task is worthy of consideration. If we determine it is important to start it as soon as possible, we snap our fingers.

MOMENTUM IS A RESULT OF ACCOUNTABILITY

As previously discussed, Accountability and Momentum are intertwined. Accountability is keeping your commitments to people. A commitment is "No Matter What." There are *tactical and relational commitments.* Tactical commitments are transactional and involve tasks. They are spoken and agreed upon. A tactical commitment might be agreeing to have a sales report on your boss's desk by 10:00 a.m. Thursday.

Relational commitments contribute to a relationship. They are usually unspoken and naturally taken on by a leader. Leaders do not have to be senior business individuals. They can be people at any level of an organization. They can also be parents, friends, and community members. A relational commitment might be a commitment to live your values, a commitment to discover and lead people to their potential, or a commitment to stand by people in times of need. Relational commitments comprise what accountability truly is.

Managing the tactical is easier when we understand and manage our relational commitments. When we master both, we build relationships, develop personal accountability, and position ourselves to create massive Momentum in our lives.

SNAP is the key to increasing productivity by prioritizing our tactical responsibilities and helping us focus on our relational commitments so we can also fulfill those. SNAP helps us get the tactical responsibilities done so that we have the time and energy to focus on our relational commitments, which create accountability in our lives and allow us to fully reach our potential.

SNAP is a commitment we make to being accountable to ourselves. It is a commitment to the principle of "No Matter What!" We snap, and we begin the task. We can only put off projects that only meet the qualification of significant for so long before we need to have a conversation with ourselves in the mirror. We can achieve at a significantly higher level if only we allow ourselves to do so.

PRIORITIZING WITH SNAP

When we have projects in front of us, we know we must start. And now that we have figured out how to start, the question becomes, where do we start? With so many items on the list of to-dos, it becomes confusing to determine the first task we focus on. Sometimes, we simply start with something easy just to get it done. But if this task is

Accountability is keeping your commitments to people.

unnecessary or not a priority, we could sabotage ourselves. Often, a big chunk of time might be lost trying to figure out the answer to this very question. So, how do we know where to start?

The answer is quite simple, really. Certain aspects of SNAP are more time-sensitive than others, such as necessity and priority. The primary quality of a task that indicates that this must be the one we start first is that it is necessary. These tasks often have a deadline and must be completed before proceeding with the others. Regardless of whether a report we must submit is insignificant to us and not a priority, we need to get started on it if it is due tomorrow.

But what if it might seem unachievable to us? The truth is, if we really want to get something done, we will figure out how to do it. If we know that it is necessary to get something done on time, we will figure out ways to make it achievable. All we need to do is start. Ideas will come to us. We may solicit help. We may seek advice. Over time, we can slowly chip away and finish the project we previously thought was unachievable. If we have multiple tasks that are necessary, we look for the ones that are also a priority, for these are the ones that we personally require ourselves to complete.

Once we have completed our necessary tasks, it becomes time to turn our attention to the tasks that are a priority. It really matters to us to complete the task by a certain time, so we must ensure it is done.

Here comes the part that is initially surprising but becomes simple once we understand it. What do we pursue when we only have either significant or achievable projects in front of us? Think back to what we spoke about when considering necessary projects. When we really want to do something, we figure out how to get it done. We need to go after the projects that are significant to us, regardless of whether they seem initially achievable or not. We must start and devote some

If we know that
it is necessary to
get something
done on time,
we will figure out
ways to make
it achievable.

energy to ensuring we try our best to achieve these projects. This does not mean, however, that we aimlessly pursue every single idea that comes into our head. This means that we reasonably attempt to work on the project before determining whether it is achievable.

As you can see, effectively prioritizing involves first ensuring that your tactical commitments are taken care of. This gives you the time to focus on your relational commitments—the significant ones—that really change your life and those around you.

THE NEXT STEP

We know why we do not start projects, why we procrastinate, and why projects are important to complete. We also now know that if we snap our fingers, we commit to starting a specific task on our list. Knowing that once we start a task, we are likely to continue on that task, build Momentum on that task, and create Momentum on a bigger scale in our lives to drive our desire to commit to SNAP. Your challenge now is to pick one thing you know you must do today, snap your fingers, and get started!

In the next section, we discuss some of the natural barriers to your Momentum and how to overcome them.

Sometimes, you have to do what you have to do, so you get to do what you want to do.

4

OVERCOMING BARRIERS TO YOUR MOMENTUM

Consistent
Action

Defeating
Limiting Beliefs

Reaction to
Distraction

THE ART OF CONSISTENCY

HAVING IDENTIFIED what projects to start and how to start them, the question becomes, how do we persevere and continue working on them? We need to ensure that we do not give up halfway through—that we continue working and pushing forward until what we set out to achieve is achieved. How do we ensure that starting any endeavor means something—that it culminates toward achieving a powerful goal?

This is where the next part of our Momentum equation comes into play. This is consistency. Consistency is what makes your growth exponential. It powers your growth so that every time you make a conscious movement toward your goal, the outcome is greater than what came before it. The second time you work toward something, its results will be better than the first. The results will be better the third time than the second, and so forth.

Consistency makes your growth exponential.

The Power Of Consistent Action

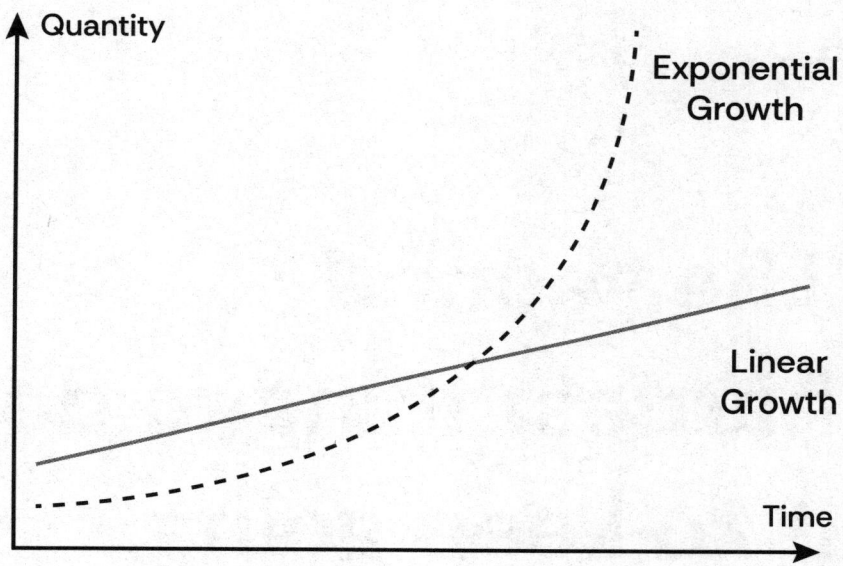

But how do we do this? How can we be consistent? We start by remembering something we discovered earlier on. The easiest thing to do is to do nothing. The hardest thing to do is to start. The second easiest thing to do is to stop. The second hardest thing to do is to keep going. This tells us that we have already done the hardest part by starting. What we must do—keep going—takes merely a fraction of the energy that was needed to start.

If we stop now, then we know that we inevitably have to start again at some point. And when we do have to start, we will once again face the hardest thing—starting. So it makes no sense to stop. We need to recognize this and realize that by being consistent, we avoid having to do the hardest thing all over again. Consistency is all about understanding this.

The second hardest thing to do is to keep going, and the second easiest thing to do is to stop.

Consistency is living the values that we identified for ourselves. We must live our values in every action and decision we take. And we need to make this a habit. When we make living our values a habit, every decision or action we make aligns with what we deeply believe in. Thus, our consistency becomes powered by our values. When our actions align with our values, it becomes far easier to actually do what we want and need to do. That is the importance of ensuring that we live our values.

When we are consistent, Momentum actually starts to take place. Remember that Momentum is speed and ease; these qualities arise when we continually move in a certain direction. The keyword here is *continually*. It is about continuous, constant movement; without consistency, our actions are isolated and not connected to any deeper purpose or meaning. Starting and stopping does not lead to Momentum. That behavior only leads to frustration, anxiety, and getting bogged down, which is the exact opposite of Momentum.

Let's say you want to walk 10,000 steps a day. You think about this for a while before you finally start and walk 10,000 steps. You just did the hardest thing—you started. The very next day, you are faced with your first challenge: Can you walk 10,000 steps two days in a row? You continue to walk 10,000 steps a day for the entire week. Now, that is a job well done.

However, the challenge on Monday is that you have a meeting with your boss, two of your top clients need personal attention, and your youngest child is home from school sick. Will you let the streak of days you have walked 10,000 steps stop?

This is a real moment of truth. Maybe you tell yourself you have a super busy day, and sometimes things just happen. Maybe you convince yourself you need an off day to let your body rest. Or maybe

Starting and stopping does not lead to Momentum.

after your day ends, your child is in bed asleep, your partner is sitting on the sofa taking care of something, and you slip out and go for a walk to get the rest of your 10,000 steps in.

At the same time, remember to set realistic expectations. Your friend Bob might walk 20,000 steps every day because he has been a marathon runner his entire life. That does not mean your goal is to eventually take on 20,000 steps as well. Maybe all you need to do is 5,000 steps every other day. Because what works for your friend might not work for you. For someone else who has not been getting any exercise, just walking for five minutes might be a great accomplishment! Remember to be realistic and kind to yourself. We do not measure a fish's worth by judging its ability to climb a tree. So set what works for you, and do it regularly.

We need to recognize the importance of consistency to be consistent. Every time you feel like stopping, remind yourself how much energy it takes to start again. Remind yourself that what you are facing right now is just the second hardest thing; and if you stop, you have to face the hardest thing again.

Another word for *consistency* is routine or habit. No one can make you do something you do not want to do. No one can force you to create a new habit.

I have always struggled with my email. Hundreds and hundreds of emails would build up in my in-box. I wasn't using email as a communication tool. It had become my to-do box. The only problem, I wasn't very good at getting to-done what was in my to-do box. I even hired an assistant to help sort and organize my email. That did not help either. Finally after years of having hundreds, if not thousands of emails that needed dealt with, something changed in me. I decided it was not acceptable to operate in that manner.

I tried a few times to focus on getting email cleaned up but did not succeed. Then one day I decided that was the day I would master my email. I spent the entire day dealing with email. I turned some emails into tasks that I wanted to complete. I archived some emails. I deleted a lot of emails. And eventually my in-box was totally empty. Now I work every day to make sure that I answer or deal with every email that comes in. I want to keep my clean in-box.

Once you develop a routine and then you break it, you miss it. What routines or habits would you like to develop in your life either personally or professionally that you would work to maintain? Internalize the Significance of those habits, the impact it will have on you and/or the people around you, and then snap your fingers.

Lack of consistency is the first barrier to success. When we recognize the importance of consistency and work toward it, we will see the true power of Momentum in action.

OVERCOMING RESISTANCE

Now that we understand the importance of consistency and have begun to make consistent, conscious movements toward our goals, we might sometimes feel like there are other barriers stopping us from getting where we want to be. They hinder our progress and, oftentimes, act like a speed bump on our journey. This is where the last part of the Momentum equation comes into play: Resistance.

Momentum = (Significance * Action) *Consistency* – Resistance

Resistance takes many forms and shapes. Yet, it always acts against our Momentum. The key to achieving good Momentum and ensuring that we remain consistent lies in our efforts to overcome and minimize the Resistance that we face. However, the solution is not a one-size-fits-all. Each of us faces our own unique forms of Resistance, and we need to work to combat them in different ways. Now, let's look at the most common forms of Resistance, the barriers to success we all face.

SELF-IMPOSED LIMITING BELIEFS

Self-imposed limiting beliefs create a significant barrier to our Momentum. These are the beliefs that we have about ourselves that lead us to underestimate or limit us from achieving our true potential. They stop us from even trying, for when we believe that we will inevitably fail, there is no point in even starting. These beliefs also push us to quit at every single obstacle we face because we think that we are not good enough to overcome them, so why even continue?

Our self-imposed limiting beliefs take numerous forms. Sometimes they manifest as imposter syndrome, where we believe that we do not belong and are simply pretending to be as good as everyone else. They also often take the form of the Big Excuse we discussed earlier. More often than not, our Big Excuse is a self-imposed limiting belief, such as "I'm not skilled enough," "I'm not good enough," or, "I can't do this."

Lack of consistency is the first barrier to success.

The key step to overcoming these beliefs is to first identify them for what they are: self-imposed beliefs. They are nothing more than manifestations of our confused and apprehensive thoughts. While we may really feel these things, these beliefs are not reality, and we are the only one who thinks these things about ourselves. We must constantly remind ourselves that we are where we are for a reason. We are not alone; everyone has negative thoughts, but these thoughts and beliefs are merely not true.

To help us realize this, try to integrate a support system of people into your life who help you become the best version of yourself. I call this the Accountability Circle™; it is a group of people who ensure that we stay aligned with our values, continue working toward our Purpose, and do not fall to our Big Excuse. This mutually benefiting circle of accountability will help you remember that you are not alone.

We are not alone; everyone has negative thoughts, but these thoughts and beliefs are merely not true.

Once we realize our self-imposed beliefs and consistently remind ourselves of our potential, it becomes easier to overcome them and unlock our potential. This practice is so important that I created an entire book and implementation manual based on it. You will find a more detailed guide in the book, *The Accountability Circle*.

SAYING YES TO EVERYTHING

Another obstacle to achieving Momentum is saying *yes* to everything and everyone. When asked for favors or help from those around them, most people go out of their way to do so. And this is something I totally understand. I like helping people! But I can't say *yes* to everyone because that means that I am forced to say *no* to everything. If I commit to every person or opportunity that comes my way, I will have no time to commit wholeheartedly to what is really important. This makes it impossible for my word to be my bond, and that is a commitment to myself and those around me that I cannot forgo.

This does not mean you say *no* every time you are asked for help. This means you consider and value your own time as much as you value others. Also, remember that "no" right now does not mean "no" forever. Complete what you have to right now, and circle back to that person who needed your assistance.

CONFLICTING PRIORITIES

What about conflicting priorities? The kind of tasks that pop up when you least expect them and throw a wrench into the works.

Consider this: I have a report due at 12 noon that takes about an hour to complete. So I decide to start at 10:30 a.m. to give myself some extra time. But my boss tells me at 10:30 that there is an emergency meeting I have to attend at 11 a.m. Now, I am left without enough time to complete the report, and I am also unable to focus on the meeting because the report is in the back of my mind.

Who is at fault here? Is it my boss who suddenly assigned me a meeting without prior information? No. I am at fault here. It is my responsibility to schedule my time in a way that manages unanticipated events like these. I put myself into a corner by not giving myself enough time to be flexible.

My Momentum toward completing the report was disrupted due to my lack of planning, not because of my conflicting priorities with my boss. To overcome this, I need to remember to plan ahead, snap, get things done, and stop waiting till the last moment possible or even close to that moment. I must remember that interruptions and other important people's priorities will impact me from time to time. This is a reality of life.

DISTRACTIONS

The last but perhaps most frequent barrier to Momentum is distractions. There are distractions all around us. These could be social media notifications, a new movie you want to watch, or even a friend texting you. Sometimes distractions also come under a productive disguise—perhaps you want to spend your time setting up a fancy new planning system rather than doing the tasks that you already have due for today. You think you are being productive, but you are just being distracted.

Many times, distractions also result from our hobbies. Personally, as an avid skier, the moment I come across a new piece of gear on the internet, it becomes highly likely that I spend the next hour reading product reviews and looking through potential skiing gear to buy. I convince myself that this is productive, as I need to buy a new helmet anyway. However, the truth is I wasted time doing something that was not significant, necessary, or a priority at the moment.

How do we deal with these distractions? Do we try to force ourselves never to fall for them or spend time on them? Or do we try to create an environment without these distractions? Well, the answer is neither. Forcing ourselves to focus might lead to burnout in the long run. Creating a distraction-free environment might work, but only as long as we are in the environment. We might fall to them all over again when we step outside of that environment.

The answer is that we should schedule our distractions. When we schedule something, it is no longer a distraction. We schedule distractions for a time when it is appropriate. We ensure that our work and responsibilities are satisfied, and now we have something to look forward to. Distractions can sometimes act as an incentive when handled properly. They could be the carrot on our stick. So, we should schedule and use our distractions wisely.

When we schedule something, it is no longer a distraction.

IMPATIENCE

Most of the time, we get frustrated when it takes too long to see results. For example, a good friend of mine was studying German. I asked him how it was going and he said, "I have been studying for three months now, and I can barely string more than a sentence together without having to pause and think. And on some days, I feel like no matter how hard I try, I learn nothing new. I feel stuck, and I feel like

Momentum is the dessert you get to eat after sweating the entire day in the kitchen preparing the meal.

my efforts are going to waste." This is a situation I am sure all of us can relate to, whether training for a marathon, trying to attract new customers, working out at the gym, or learning the guitar.

We are often impatient to see results, and that leads to frustration, which causes us to stop prematurely. We need to remember that Momentum is not the struggle we are currently feeling. Momentum is the dessert you get to eat after sweating the entire day in the kitchen preparing the meal. And if we want the dessert, then we need to spend the time making it.

Sometimes it helps to break our goals into smaller tasks so we can feel a consistent sense of progress. Through doing so, we can see how each step we take brings us closer to achieving our goals. It helps us enjoy the process. At the same time, it is important to remember that the big win is always right around the corner. You just cannot see it yet. Do not quit early, and understand that it takes time. Good things always take time, and it is up to us to give ourselves the time we need to get there.

WHO IS IN CHARGE?

I have an office and studio where I work from home. Sometimes I take my laptop into the kitchen, where my wife, Renee, is maybe doing something. I realized something the other day, and I asked Renee, "Do you know the difference between me working in my office or me working up here?" Renee shrugged her shoulders. I responded, "When I work in my office, I'm distracted by YouTube. When I work up here, I'm distracted by you."

There will always be barriers to our Momentum. How we see those barriers, how we react to them, and how we eliminate those barriers are decisions we must make.

As I think about this, I realize that neither YouTube nor Renee was distracting me. I was allowing something or someone to distract me. It was up to me. I was giving up control of what I did and how I did it.

There will always be barriers to our Momentum. How we see those barriers, how we react to them, and how we eliminate those barriers are decisions we must make. We decide, we commit, and then we move forward. It always comes down to a choice, and the choice is always ours to make.

When we understand that we are going to face barriers to Momentum, we will naturally prepare for those moments. Moving past all of these barriers ensures we are living with Momentum. Now we need to create a full life of Momentum.

5

LIVING A LIFE OF MOMENTUM AND ACCOUNTABILITY

Sustaining Momentum

Minimizing Resistance

Appreciating the Adventure of Life

SUSTAINING MOMENTUM

ONCE WE START and build Momentum, the question automatically becomes, how do we keep it going? How do we sustain our Momentum? Sustaining Momentum in our life provides us continuous forward movement and helps us create and live a life of accountability.

We need to start by realizing that pursuing our goals is an uphill journey, and while it may be more steep than usual or less steep than usual, it is always uphill. Life never becomes easier to climb. However, if we consistently keep climbing, we get better at it. And if we do it for long enough, we happen to come across a car on the way. This car is Momentum. The car does not run on its own, nor does it run immediately. We have to push it up the hill for a while, and this is the extremely hardest part. But soon enough, we find that the car turns on with the fuel of our efforts.

Once the car starts running, the journey uphill is exponentially easier. But we need to remember to fuel it with our effort, energy, and focus. The moment we stop and slack off, the car breaks down. And then we are forced to endure the hardest part yet again: we have to continue our journey on foot for a while before we find another car, which requires us to exert all our energy to push it for a while before it turns on again.

The key to sustaining Momentum and continually climbing the hill is to ensure that we keep the car running. We do not let it stop, and we take care of it with everything we have.

Many times the first voice is one of doubt. People are very quick to tell us what we cannot do, including ourselves. We need to learn to drown out those voices and surround ourselves with the voice of support, the voice that tells us we can do it, and the voice that encourages us to be our best. This is the voice that says we can do more, we can achieve at a level beyond what we ourselves probably thought was impossible, but in reality is very possible. We just do not know it is possible yet. We have not figured out how to do that yet. But through creating Momentum we will figure it out.

There is no doubt. You are in motion. There is no such thing as standing still. You are moving toward something. You are moving toward your goals or you are moving away from them. And everyone around you is also in motion. You either create positive Momentum, or you create negative Momentum. You get to choose. Knowing how to SNAP and create positive Momentum positions you to create a life of infinite possibilities.

PULLING IT TOGETHER

In essence, Momentum does not manifest in our life by itself. It takes effort and energy to achieve Momentum and become like those people in our lives who look like they can accomplish everything they want effortlessly. However, at the same time, Momentum is not impossible to achieve. It just takes time, reflection, and most importantly, a commitment to ourselves.

Remembering that Momentum is a result of four different elements can help us focus our efforts in attaining it.

Sustaining Momentum in our life provides us continuous forward movement and helps us create and live a life of accountability.

Momentum = (Significance * Action) ^{Consistency} - Resistance

We began by understanding how to identify the things that are truly significant to us. Things that really mean something to our identity, and will help us unlock Momentum. To understand our true aspirations and goals, we need to first understand ourselves. We need to understand our Why, What, and How to begin our journey. After all, a ship lost at sea is in a much worse situation than one stuck at the harbor its entire life. But we do not want to be either. Through reflection and questioning ourselves, we need to identify our Purpose, Mission, and Values and determine our destination before beginning the journey. This will fuel us with the sense of direction imperative to Momentum.

Having completed this, the toughest part lies ahead of us: actually starting. This corresponds to the second part of the Momentum equation: Action. Taking action—starting—is the hardest thing to do.

Most often, one of the biggest problems stopping us from starting is just the sheer number of tasks we have to complete, and the confusion that arises when trying to decide what to do first. The SNAP framework helps us do exactly that—decide and start. Using it, we can identify exactly what to start on, snap and start. It relies on a commitment to ourselves—a commitment to the SNAP.

An integral key to Momentum is consistency. It is not about isolated moments of working toward our goals, but instead is about continuously and consciously progressing toward what we want to achieve. As we have learned, the principle that allows us to become consistent lies in our realization that starting again is going to become infinitely more difficult than simply continuing to push forward. The potential of consistency in allowing Momentum to grow exponentially is key in helping us become the best version of ourselves.

Finally, it also becomes necessary for us to overcome and minimize the negative factor reducing our Momentum: Resistance. Resistance is integrally present in all of our lives, in the form of distractions, fears, worries, confusion, and more. Each type of Resistance requires a unique strategy, and employing it accordingly to overcome these barriers is what helps us truly achieve Momentum.

Through Momentum, we become a truly accountable person. It helps us stay on Purpose, work toward what we care about, and fulfill our commitments to those around us. More importantly, it allows us to create a positive change in the lives of others, and be a dedicated, reliable, and inspiring person.

Momentum is constant, conscious movement toward your goal that is in alignment with your Purpose and Mission.

The principles of moving effortlessly toward your goals can be applied anywhere and anytime, despite where you are in life. You could be in high school aiming for good grades, in your early career looking to get that job promotion, a business owner wanting to create change in their local neighborhood! All it takes is a few minutes of reflection to start. Identify your Big Three, realize the power of the "we" mindset, apply the SNAP framework, minimize your Resistance and get started! It will blow your mind just how much you can achieve once you put your mind to it, and unlock the power of Momentum.

REMEMBERING TO BREATHE

On his 60th wedding anniversary, my father told me something that has stuck with me ever since.

"Sam. Life is an adventure. Go live the adventure."

At that moment, I thought he meant for me to keep going forward and achieving new things. To experiment, grow, improve, and keep adventuring. But a while later, it struck me that his words had a bigger meaning. I realized that I might have misunderstood the adventure to just be the thrilling parts that filled me up with adrenaline like running marathons or hiking up mountains.

Adventures are also about the preparation, the anxiety of actually doing it, the resting periods in between, the journey back home once it's over, and maybe most importantly, the people we share these experiences with. Like he said, life is an adventure—every single part of life is an adventure, not just the exciting bits but the boring and tiring parts too.

You either create positive Momentum, or you create negative Momentum. You get to choose.

Renee and I enjoy skiing in the winter. I came to notice that Renee seemed to continuously lag behind me. Renee can ski nicely, and I wondered why I was always ahead of her. Finally, one day, I skied for a few moments and then stopped, turned around, and saw Renee stop to take in the view. It did not take me long to realize that getting to the bottom was not what brought Renee joy on her journey. What Renee really loved was stopping on the side of the mountain and taking in the views and the majesty of it all. The breathtaking view was what Renee wanted, what brought joy to her adventure, and what I learned to also love.

Oftentimes in life, we get so caught up in the act of "doing"— completing reports, reading emails, preparing for presentations, working, cooking, cleaning, driving to the office—that we forget to simply "be." Life's adventure is also about being. What we strive to achieve—to positively impact the lives of those around us—can only be truly enjoyed when we learn to appreciate being.

To realize the fruits of our labor, we must sometimes stop and breathe it all in. We need to enjoy it, regardless of where we are. People often say life is about the journey, not the destination, but I disagree. I say it's about both! Life is the frequent stops you make on your way to the destination. Life is those moments when you look around and realize just how far you have come and celebrate that progress. And more often than not, life shines through loudest in those quiet moments of reflection. We need to remember to celebrate the small wins, for the big wins are nothing but the culmination of the former!

We must prioritize our mental and physical health to truly enjoy everything we work for. And sometimes, we need to stop when we realize that enough is enough. There is no need to push ourselves to achieve things for the sole sake of achieving them. Our journey should be powered by a desire to make a positive change, not to be better than everyone else.

If we are happy where we are and happy with the impact we have on those around us, it is okay to stop. Stop and breathe it all in. Reflect on how far you have come and how much you have changed. Take that moment to yourself. This moment might be a few seconds, minutes, days, or even months. One of the biggest parts of the adventure of life are these moments.

So remember to value these moments equally. It is as important as scaling the mountain to take some rest periodically and celebrate your impact. Take care of your mind, your body, and your soul as much as you take care of your work and all that you try to achieve. Recall that Momentum is continuous, constant movement toward your goal and part of creating and living an accountable life. Resting on the way is an integral part of the journey. Resting and taking time for yourself is not a break from Momentum. It is part of Momentum.

So, now it's up to you.

Where do you start?

SNAP!

About the Author

SAM SILVERSTEIN is recognized globally as an accountability and leadership expert. Global Gurus consistently names him as one of the World's Top 30 Organizational Culture Professionals. He is the author of 13 books including: *No More Excuses; The Accountability Advantage; Pivot!; The Accountability Circle; I Am Accountable; No Matter What; Non-Negotiable; Making Accountable Decisions;* and *The Success Model.*

Keynote speaker Sam Silverstein is the founder of The Accountability Institute™ and the Certified Accountability Advisor™. Sam hosts Accountability Roundtables™ to address and break through barriers that restrict organizations and communities from living an accountable culture.

Originally from Atlanta, Georgia, Sam earned a Bachelor's degree in business from the University of Georgia and an MBA from Washington University. He is a past president of the National Speakers Association. Sam has been inducted into the Council of Peers Award for Excellence (CPAE) Speakers Hall of Fame. He is married with four children and currently resides in St. Louis, Missouri.

FOR MORE INFORMATION VISIT:

samsilverstein.com

For free tools and resources to build accountability
and momentum in your life, go to:

WWW.ISNAP.IO

BOOK SAM SILVERSTEIN
TO SPEAK AT YOUR NEXT EVENT

Contact Us

Sam Silverstein, Incorporated
121 Bellington Lane
St. Louis, Missouri 63141
info@SamSilverstein.com
(314) 878-9252

To Order More Copies of
MOMENTUM

www.samsilverstein.com

Follow Sam

www.twitter.com/samsilverstein

www.youtube.com/samsilverstein

www.linkedin.com/in/samsilverstein

www.instagram.com/samsilverstein

www.facebook.com/silversteinsam

OTHER BOOKS BY SAM SILVERSTEIN

The Theory of Accountability | The Accountability Circle | The Accountability Advantage

No More Excuses | Making Accountable Decisions | The Success Model | I Am Accountable

No Matter What | The Lost Commandments | Non Negotiable | Pivot!